Dear Daughter

Dear Daughter

DENISE GEORGE

BROADMAN PRESS
Nashville, Tennessee

© Copyright 1985 • Broadman Press
All rights reserved
4256-63
ISBN: 0-8054-5663-5
Dewey Decimal Classification: 306.8
Subject Headings: MOTHERS // PARENT AND CHILD
Library of Congress Catalog Card Number: 85-15145
Printed in the United States of America

Unless otherwise noted, all Scripture quotations are from the Revised
Standard Version of the Bible, copyrighted 1946, 1952, © 1971, 1973.

Scripture quotations marked (KVJ) are from the King James Version of
the Bible.

Library of Congress Cataloging in Publication Data

George, Denise.
    Dear daughter.

    1. Mothers and daughters—Meditations. I. Title.
BV4847.G46 1985   242'.6431   85-15145
ISBN 0-8054-5663-5

For my daughter

Alyce Elizabeth

Acknowledgments

My sincere gratitude goes to Wayne E. Oates, who, through a course in pastoral counseling at Southern Baptist Theological Seminary, spawned many of the ideas about which I have written.

As always, to my husband, Timothy George, who remains my strongest, most encouraging supporter, and, who, through his own career and hard work, allows me the freedom to study and write, I am deeply and lovingly indebted.

Finally, to my children, Christian Timothy and Alyce Elizabeth, who add a unique and joyous dimension to my life—that of motherhood—and who sleep so soundly in the early morning and late night hours that I may write, I pledge my everlasting devotion.

DENISE GEORGE
Louisville, Kentucky
August 16, 1984

Preface

Dear Alyce,

This is your book. Within these pages lies a collection of letters to you, Alyce Elizabeth, my dear daughter.

I began writing these letters to you on the day you came into this world—August 16, 1983. I have finished the book on the day of your first birthday.

You will find these letters very personal. They capture some of your mother's more tender, private thoughts as well as her hopes, dreams, and prayers for you. More than once, I have recalled time-worn and treasured remembrances from my childhood. I share with you freely my joys and sorrows, my regrets and fears, my laughter and tears.

I rejoiced the moment I found out that you, my second child, would be a daughter. Before you were born, I had already discovered the adventures of motherhood through your two-year-old brother, Christian. He and I, mother and son, have always had a special love for each other. I knew that you and I would also know an endearing love. I felt, however, that our relationship would be somewhat different from his and mine. For you and I share a unique understanding, a oneness, a common bond—that of being born female.

I pray, Alyce, that this book will hold deep meaning for you. It is written from the heart of a joyous mother whom God has blessed with a dear daughter.

Love,
Mother

Contents

1

You As a Woman

"Female He created them.
And God saw . . . that . . . it was very good"
(Gen. 1:27, 31, KJV).

Dear Daughter

Dear Alyce,

The year was 1906. A lovely young mother (my great-grandmother), dressed in an ankle-length dress, stood with her five small children posing for the photographer. All of her little ones wore handmade white cotton outfits, neatly starched and pressed. Beautifully handmade clothes, happy children, a grateful mother—what a lovely picture they made.

One of those children in the photograph, a little twin girl, was your great-grandmother, Alice Crane. She would grow up and marry the boy down the street, George Williams. Their marriage, which would be blessed with three children, six grandchildren, and, with your birth, nine great-grandchildren, would last until her death in 1983—64 years.

Alice Crane Williams was a lovely, caring, dedicated Christian woman. I called her Mama. You will read much about Mama throughout these letters, Alyce, for she had a great influence on my life.

You bear her name, *Alyce.*

Let me introduce you to another fine Christian woman, your father's great-aunt, Mary Elizabeth George. A widow, she had no children of her own.

The year was 1950. Your father, only three months old, needed a home. Aunt Mary, already into her sixties, took him into her home, loved him, and reared him just like her own son.

Even though I never knew her well, I loved Aunt Mary. She died a few years after your father and I married. I do know of the great influence she had on your father's life and of his deep love for her. Mary Elizabeth George was a devoted Christian woman who gave herself to others unselfishly.

You bear her name, *Elizabeth.*

Be grateful to God, Alyce, for Mama and Aunt Mary. Wear their names with great thanksgiving. For you are a part of these two women, and a part of many other loved ones so long ago lost from memory.

Love,
Mother

My Prayer for You

Dear Father,

For Alice Crane Williams and Mary Elizabeth George, I give You thanks. May Alyce Elizabeth possess their love and compassion, devotion and strength. May she be sincerely grateful to these two women who were so dedicated to You and to their families.

In Jesus' name,
Amen.

A Mother's Love

Dear Alyce,

Last week, a baby blue jay fell out of its nest and into our backyard. A tiny creature, it was much too small to fly. We watched as the mother blue jay swooped down to examine her baby's situation. Since she could not return it to her home in the tree, she determined it would just have to grow into adolescence on the ground.

We walked out every day, Alyce, and checked on the baby bird. Not far above us, at all times, a concerned mother hovered, springing from branch to branch, ready to pounce on us if we disturbed her baby. When we moved out of sight, she would once again go to it, feed it, and care for it.

Most mothers are like that mother blue jay, Alyce. I believe that nature provides a mother with a strong "love" instinct for her baby. She nurtures, cares for, and protects her child. Aside from God's love for His children, what could be more precious than a mother's love?

I love you like that, Alyce. I am devoted to you. I can never imagine a time when I won't love you. You are my child, and in that fact I take loving pride and great responsibility.

The mother blue jay's devotion to her baby continued for five days. She fed it, guarded it, and stayed close by its side. Then one day, we went to look for the baby bird, and it was gone. We searched the yard but recovered no bird. We feared that the baby bird had become a victim of some unkind predator.

Up in the tree, we heard a rustling of leaves. The mother blue jay sat on a limb high above us, staring at us, and gazing at the ground, also looking for the tiny bird.

No doubt, she still springs from branch to branch, by day and by night, searching for her baby.

Love,
Mother

My Prayer for You

Dear Father,

Thank You for the love You have given me for my children. May

I always be close by them, caring for them, protecting them, and loving them.

In His love, I pray,
Amen.

The Truly Beautiful Woman

Dear Alyce,

Let me tell you a very sad story about a woman named Virginie Avegno. She was part French and part Italian. Born in Louisiana, she married a French banker. Legend says she was so exquisitely beautiful that she stopped traffic in the streets. Ludwig II of Bavaria once traveled all the way to Paris just to watch her walk up the grand staircase of the Opera House. In 1884, when Virginie Avegno was twenty-four years old, John Singer Sargent painted her portrait. The painter who did not adequately capture her beauty on canvas, had to flee the city due to the uproar his portrait caused.

Virginie's beauty made her famous. One day, however, as she walked along the beach at Cannes, she overheard a woman say that she was beginning to look worn. Virginie was so upset by the woman's critical statement, she at once drove to her hotel in a closed carriage. She took a private compartment on the train to Paris. She spent the rest of her life in shuttered rooms without mirrors. One could only see her as she walked the beach by her country house—at midnight.

This is a somewhat extreme story, Alyce, but it does make a point.

How different Virginie Avegno's life might have been had she not been quite so beautiful. How different Virginie Avengo's life might have been had she not lived only for her beauty.

As with Virginie, outward beauty fades. No woman can remain forever young. The fountain of youth does not exist. But one kind of beauty does last forever. Inner beauty, the kind that grows and develops as the years pass, can make a woman truly beautiful. Even though the face muscles may sag a bit, a few wrinkles may appear, and the hair lightens to gray, the charm that comes from within deepens each year and produces a beauty that no youth could ever know.

Concentrate on that inner beauty, Alyce. Let it shine through you. Develop it, for the more it grows the more you glow. In doing so, you won't mind when one day you begin to look "somewhat worn." You'll never know the burden of trying to keep a maturing body eternally teenage. Grow old with grace, Alyce, and be a beautiful inspiration for all who look upon you to behold.

Love,
Mother

My Prayer for You

Abba,

Help my daughter to be a truly beautiful woman. Fill her with love for You and with love for Your children everywhere. May the inner beauty she receives from You remain with her for a lifetime.

In Christ's name,
Amen.

Your Magnificent Obsession

Dear Alyce,

I hope you will discover very early in your life your "niche"— your *magnificent obsession*! What is a magnificent obsession? It's your dream, perhaps your fantasy, something you enjoy doing or only hope to do. It is something deep down in your heart that, if you dare to follow your dream, may very well obsess you and demand an equal share of your day.

You may spend a lifetime looking for your niche. Or, you may find it early in your life. You will long for it even before you know what "it" is. When you discover your magnificent obsession, you'll know it.

One author states it this way: "When you have found your 'niche' in life, it becomes a haven of rest, a source of security, and a freedom from restlessness to you. It becomes to you as the orbits of stars and planets are to them, a destiny, not a fate or doom. Your sense of destiny provides you with an inner serenity that no one can take from you but yourself."[1]

Seek to discover, Alyce, what you are called to do, your destiny in life, your reason for being alive. Your magnificent obsession will enhance your life, will give you self-esteem, will deliver you from boredom, will bring you (and perhaps many others) much joy, and will fill your days for the rest of your life.

Perhaps your magnificent obsession will be children. If so, put yourself into rearing, teaching, and loving children with all your strength. Direct your energies toward them, whether they are your own, your best friend's, or unseen little ones in every corner of the world who need you.

Perhaps your magnificent obsession will be social justice. If so, find a needful cause (they abound on every hand) and work hard to liberate minorities, stamp out world hunger and poverty, stop spouse and child abuse, eliminate drug and alcohol abuse—whatever you can do to make this world a more just place to live.

Perhaps your magnificent obsession will be running or swimming or skiing or any number of physical exercises or sports. Perhaps it will be working with the elderly or the handicapped. Maybe you will love books, like your father, and will use every spare moment, day and night, to read, to learn, and to teach others what you've learned.

You already know my magnificent obsession. *Writing!* I live and breathe my next devotional, article, and book. Few things could entice me from my warm bed at 4:30 in the morning while everyone else sleeps or could detain me from my bed long after everyone has said good night. With a cup of coffee in hand, I write at my desk each day, watching the sun either come up or set through the leaves of the big oak tree in our backyard.

I write for several reasons: primarily to declare and share my faith in and my love for Jesus Christ, to help others who face the same crises that I, myself, have faced, and, through devotional material, to uplift and encourage people in life's commonplace situations. The Lord has given me a love for words and the burning desire to use those words in His work.

Alyce, may your magnificent obsession be like mine—a vital part of life. For me to *live* is to *write.* I cannot *not* write. (Only another writer could understand the fervor of that feeling!) If I were to stop writing, I would feel like the prophet Jeremiah who could not refrain from his divine proclamation: "If I say, 'I will not mention Him, or speak any more in His name,' " Jeremiah admitted, "there is in my heart as it were a burning fire shut up in my bones, and I am weary with holding it in, and I cannot" (Jer. 20:9).

I know of that fire—that consuming and all encompassing fire—shut up in my bones. It burns both day and night and demands that I put words on paper.

Whatever your niche in life, Alyce, learn of it. I will help you discover what it is. Work hard at it and love your work, for work that is pleasurable is not really *work* at all! If you can make your magnificent obsession your life's career, as I have, and earn some, if not all, of your livelihood from it, all the better. Dare to dream, and make those dreams become reality. For if you do, perhaps you, too, will know of that fire in your heart, shut up in your bones.

Love,
Mother

My Prayer for You

O God,

I pray that Alyce will find her niche in life, her magnificent obsession. May she dream her dreams and may they become reality. I pray that You will show her, like You have shown me, her haven of rest, her source of security, and her freedom from restlessness—the inner serenity—the destiny for which she was made.

In His name, I pray,
Amen.

Leaving Home

Dear Alyce,

Wiping great drops of tears from my eyes, I took a last look out the window of the Greyhound bus and waved good-bye to my mother. The bus would take me, a ten-year-old girl, only a hundred miles away to my grandparent's home for a two-week stay. I always waited eagerly for those weeks at Mama's and Papa's, but leaving my mother, father, and sister always brought a certain sadness.

On this particular day, as the bus pulled out of the station and my mother disappeared from sight, I pondered the day in the future when I would leave home, not for two weeks, but forever.

That day finally came. It happened not when I married, for my new husband and I moved into a church pastorate within a few miles of my parent's home. But two years later, the day came.

Your father was accepted to do graduate work at Harvard Divinity School in Cambridge, Massachusetts—truly, the end of the world for us. We had never been so far from home before. We packed everything we owned and a few things we had borrowed into our old Plymouth Satelite. That night, before we went to bed, we hugged and said our farewells, as early morning good-byes would have been too painful. At 4:30 the next morning, I took a last look from the car window, and we drove off, a thousand miles into the unknown.

My time to leave home had come. Little did I know, on that early August morning in 1972, that we would live in New England for the next seven years, with only a short annual visit home. After your father's graduation, we didn't go back home. We settled in another part of the country, hundreds of miles from our families.

Your time will come too, Alyce. You will grow up and leave those who have known and loved you since your birth. For you must also begin a life independent of us. No doubt, you, too, will wipe away a tear or two as you take a last look through your own window and depart for the unknown.

Love,
Mother

My Prayer for You

Lord, we will have Alyce with us for such a short time. Help us to treasure the moments we are all together as mother, father, brother, and sister.

In Jesus' abiding love,
Amen.

A Teachable Moment

Dear Alyce,

Every now and then, often for some, seldom for others, never for a few, the heart is open and the spirit is accepting. A teachable moment occurs. This is a time of insight, of personal reflection, of learning, and of teaching.

I remember one such teachable moment that came to me when I

was pregnant with you. During the first three months of pregnancy, I experienced severe nausea. I stayed at home for many weeks in bed, hardly eating, and losing weight. My doctor finally admitted me to the hospital where I could be fed through my veins.

I can remember lying in the hospital bed late one night, listening to the sounds around me. The darkened room, the sound of the nurses' soft-soled shoes pacing the long hallways, the occasional clashing of IV bottles and bedpans, the muffled cries of the young woman, a victim of miscarriage, in the bed next to mine—all this and more plunged me into deep thought. I suddenly became aware of all the others who, like me, were bedded down in this institution of suffering. While I had felt sympathy in the past for those who suffered physically, now I could go one step further than *sympathy*. I was painfully and unwillingly taught *empathy*. I was one of them. I knew physical suffering. My teachable moment came as I lay flat on my back, hearing the groans of others comingled with my own inner groans.

Another teachable moment came to me before I married during a Christmas family get-together at my grandparent's home. During the singing of carols, the festive eating, and the gift-openings, I stepped away from myself for a moment. My body stayed in place, surrounded by grandparents, parents, sister, cousins, aunts and uncles. But my mind's eye scanned the delightfully noisy and busy room. I saw my loved ones as if for the first time. Mama, Papa, Mom, Dad, Aunt Mella, Uncle Bud, Aunt Virginia, Uncle Leon, Jill, Alan, Alicia, Ann, Cheryl—all of them became precious individuals to me, not just the family as a whole, but those loving souls with whom I had grown up, those I had come to know well and to love. Standing mentally at the sidelines, I wondered what the next years would bring. How many more Christmases would we be able to be together? I stood back from the festivities only long enough to say a prayer of thanksgiving for each member of my family and to take a moment to be aware of how fortunate we were to be together.

I have thought back to that teachable moment on many Christmas days hence. Of course, time didn't stand still. I married your father and moved a thousand miles away, making it impossible to return home to celebrate Christmas with my family. Over the years, the family members would cope with unexpected crises—divorce, severe illness, life-threatening surgery, and death. I pray that at one time or another each family member also experienced in some similar way that same moment of awareness that I met face-to-face on that Christmas afternoon.

Moments of awareness. The teachable moments of life. I believe that Jesus had many teachable moments in His brief life on earth. He knew loneliness as He faced the awesome challenge of His earthly ministry. He knew temptation as Satan came to Him and tried to make Him stumble. He knew hunger as He prayed and fasted for forty days in a wilderness. He knew alienation when His own people failed to recognize Him as the Son of God. Perhaps His greatest burden, He knew desertion, for at His death He cried out to the One whom He knew and loved the most: "My God, my God, why hast thou forsaken me?" (Matt. 27:46, KJV).

Jesus had sympathy for the great masses of suffering people. But, more importantly, the teachable moments in His life had given Him empathy.

Alyce, take time in your busy schedule to recognize teachable moments when they come to you. Treasure them. Learn from them. Remember them. I hope those moments will come often to you. Let them be your teachers about life and about those things in life that are truly important and lasting. Take time to recognize a teachable moment when it has visited another who must learn from it. Minister to those who, even for a brief moment, have been given opened hearts and accepting spirits. See yourself as being taught and also as a teacher to others. Have sympathy for those who suffer. But even greater than sympathy, let the precious teachable moments give to you the gift of empathy.

Love,
Mother

My Prayer for You

Dear Heavenly Father,

For the teachable moments You have allowed me, I am deeply grateful. I pray You will give my daughter those treasures of insight, those rare and remembered moments when her heart will be opened and her spirit accepting, those gifts of sympathy which will become gifts of empathy. When the teachable moments do come, I pray that she will be receptive to them and that she will realize that during those quiet still seconds perhaps You, Yourself, reach out and whisper in her ear.

For the gift of receiving special insights, and for the opportunities of sharing these gifts with others during their own teachable moments, may she be indebted to You, the Teacher of all good things.

In His sweet name,
Amen.

The Ideal Wife and Mother

Dear Alyce,

It's a difficult time to be a woman, especially a Christian woman. Society may tell you one thing about your place as wife and mother, and family and friends may tell you another.

Not very long ago, in the span of history, a woman's "place" was most always in the home, tending to her husband and children. By law, she could not own property. With few exceptions, she could not find work outside the home. Marriage remained almost the only financial support the woman of yesterday had.

Today, of course, women have many more options. They are working outside the home in large numbers. They are taking significant roles in our society's leadership. "Your place is at home with your children, not out in the work force," a family member may tell a new mother. But, at the same time, society, as well as other women, may be putting pressure on this mother to take a job outside the home. The Christian mother of today may be listening to all who advise her, shaking her head in confusion, and wondering what she should do.

I'm sure you will face this same question one day, Alyce. Should you work outside the home? Or, should you work totally inside the home? Or, can you have the freedom to do both? Just what *does* make the ideal wife and mother?

Listen to the description of a ideal wife in Proverbs 31:10-28.

A good wife who can find?
  She is far more precious than jewels.
The heart of her husband trusts in her,
  and he will have no lack of gain.
She does him good, and not harm
  all the days of her life.
She seeks wool and flax,
  and works with willing hands.
She is like the ships of the merchant,
  she brings her food from afar.
She rises while it is yet night
  and provides food for her household
  and tasks for her maidens.

She considers a field and buys it;
　　with the fruit of her hands she plants a vineyard.
She girds her loins with strength and makes her arms strong.
She perceives that her merchandise is profitable.
　　Her lamp does not go out at night.
She puts her hands to the distaff,
　　and her hands hold the spindle.
She opens her hand to the poor,
　　and reaches out her hands to the needy.
She is not afraid of snow for her household,
　　for all her household are clothed in scarlet.
She makes herself coverings;
　　her clothing is fine linen and purple.
Her husband is known in the gates,
　　when he sits among the elders of the land.
She makes linen garments and sells them;
　　she delivers girdles to the merchant.
Strength and dignity are her clothing,
　　and she laughs at the time to come.
She opens her mouth with wisdom,
　　and the teaching of kindness is on her tongue.
She looks well to the ways of her household,
　　and does not eat the bread of idleness.
Her children rise up and call her blessed;
　　her husband also, and he praises her.

Notice, Alyce, that this woman had the freedom to devote herself to her family, and, at the same time, to be a businesswoman. Wife, mother, taskmaster, merchant, cook, businesswoman, gardener, harvester, saleswoman, weaver, social worker, seamstress, teacher, and/or household manager. This biblical description of a woman gives us an unlimited amount of *freedom* in our choice of where and how to work.

The author of this passage in Proverbs made another statement about the ideal wife and mother. This message is perhaps even greater than the first. In all that she did, she did *joyfully*. In her homemaking and in her outside job, she kept the best interests of her family always close to her heart. She worked for the benefit of the family as a whole. She concerned herself with the needy, and reached out to them to minister, provide, and comfort. Precious, trustworthy, good, willing, strong, unafraid, dignified, joyous (laughter), wise, kind, busy (lack of idleness), and blessed—those are the words that describe her.

Alyce, one day you may marry and have children of your own. Depending on your financial situation, you may or may not have the freedom to decide whether you will work inside and/or outside your home. But if you do have a choice, make your decision prayerfully. Remember, if you choose the role of wife and mother, you must always keep the best interests of your family as a whole (and, that includes *yourself*) in mind and heart as you go about your life's work.

Love,
Mother

My Prayer for You

Lord, I pray that in all Alyce chooses she will show kindness, concern, unselfishness, generosity, and the other virtues shown by the biblical woman. May her children also rise up and call her blessed, and may her husband praise her.

In the name of our Lord,
Amen.

A Pressed Flower

Dear Alyce,

Folded within the yellowed pages of the old family Bible lies a pressed flower. It has lain undisturbed for perhaps a hundred years. The scent no longer lingers, the petals crisp with age, the color softened from the years. The flower, no doubt, holds within its folds a loving remembrance from a time long ago.

Who, I wonder, placed the flower so lovingly between the pressing pages? A young girl with a first-date corsage? A mother, saving a funeral spray's rose, as she grieved the death of her child? Could it be a wedding flower carried a century ago by a new bride? Or perhaps, a widow's last flower given to her by her husband?

We will never know.

But, Alyce, we do know that a flower so precious, so cherished by the one who placed it between the pages, need not be removed. We will leave it there, pressed in the family Bible, for your daughters and your daughter's daughters to admire and ponder.

Love,
Mother

My Prayer for You

O Lord, we thank You for a loving remembrance, a time of reflection, given to us through a pressed flower.

In His abiding love, we pray,
Amen.

A Time to Rest

Dear Alyce,

Listen to these words from Ecclesiastes 3:1-8:

For everything there is a season and a time for every matter under heaven:

a time to be born, and a time to die;

a time to plant, and a time to pluck up what is planted:

a time to kill, and a time to heal;

a time to break down, and a time to build up;

a time to weep, and a time to laugh;

a time to mourn, and a time to dance;

a time to cast away stones, and a time to gather stones together;

a time to embrace, and a time to refrain from embracing;

a time to seek, and a time to lose;

a time to keep, and a time to cast away;

a time to rend, and a time to sew;

a time to keep silence, and a time to speak;

a time to love, and a time to hate;

a time for war, and a time for peace.

These are more than just beautiful words, Alyce. Hidden in each line is a message—the message of *rest*. It would read just as true, if not as poetically, had the author written: "For everything there is a season, and a time for every matter under heaven: a time to be born, and a time to *rest* from life (death); a time to plant, and a time to *rest* from planting (harvest); a time to kill, and a time to *rest* from killing (to heal); a time to break down, and a time to *rest* from breaking down (to renew and build up again); a time to weep, and a time to *rest* from weeping (to laugh), and so on.

Read on in Ecclesiastes, Alyce, and you will discover why God gives to us the gift of rest and why He wants us to use his precious gift. "I know that there is nothing better for them than to be happy and enjoy themselves as long as they live; also that it is God's gift to man [and woman] that every one should eat and drink and take pleasure in all his [her] toil" (Eccl. 3:12-13).

Could the author be referring to *a time of rest* to help provide that happiness in toil? Indeed, to take pleasure in work, one must sometime refrain from working and seek rest and renewal.

Wayne E. Oates has written a superb book entitled *Your Right to Rest.* He writes about the "most personal renewable resource of energy you and I have, our own physical strength, stamina, and health. . . . Rest, in the harum-scarum existence of your daily life and mine, is often a low-rated function. Yet in God's creation of us and in the biblical script for the drama of a well-lived and well-ordered life, rest is something indispensable, a necessity."[2]

Dr. Oates uses the example of the work-rest rhythm of the heart which depends on a balance of beat and rest, beat and rest, beat and rest in order to function properly.[3] Think of the difference it would make in our lives and in our health, if we would follow the ways of our heart and develop such a work-rest rhythm to our lives. How much more would we take pleasure in our toil if we could anticipate a time of rest between each arduous task.

Study the words of Ecclesiastes, Alyce. Take them to heart. Accept with gladness the gift God gave you—your right to rest.

Love,
Mother

My Prayer for You

Dear Father, Giver of all perfect rest, I ask that You will encourage Alyce to take time to rest. This is, indeed, Your gift to her.

When she tires from the weight of troubles and toil, may she find in You perfect peace and perfect rest, once again knowing the happiness and pleasure You intended for her.

> In the name of the Author of perfect rest,
> Amen.

Your Body

Dear Alyce,

Let me tell you the story of a young woman.

On the night she died, she was only twenty years old. At her boyfriend's house, she placed a rifle against her head and pulled the trigger.

A young woman from the Midwest, leaving a loving church-going family, she had driven with her high-school sweetheart to Los Angeles. A youthful and innocent victim, she had become involved with the world of pornography. She posed for a number of sexually explicit magazines and made several porn movies.

During the two-year span, her family made numerous attempts in vain to reason with her and bring her back home.

A young woman of twenty, her rewards for having given her precious young body to those who would betray it, misuse it, and abuse it, were money, lovers, drugs, and death.

I tell you this story, Alyce, because this young woman was only one of a legion of girls who so freely use their bodies to achieve what they consider "success." Within a short time, they are tired and all used up. They envision the rest of their lives spent enslaved to disease, chemicals, and ruthless "lovers" who control them. The price they pay—the degrading of their bodies, the loss of dignity and self-respect, and a lifetime left without joy—is far more than they bargained for.

You have a tender young body, Alyce, healthy, strong, and active. It will serve you well for many years if you will take good care of it. Your body is far too precious to trade for what the world considers "love" or "success" or "wealth." For you have a treasure of much greater value than these, you have a healthy pure body.

Your body is far more than yours alone. The apostle Paul asked: "Do you not know that your body is a temple of the Holy Spirit within you, which you have from God? You are not your own; you were bought with a price. So glorify God in your body" (1 Cor. 6:19-20). For the Christian the Lord God, in the person of the Holy Spirit, lives within you—closer than your breathing and nearer than your hands and feet, Tennyson once wrote. That remains a responsibility you alone must bear.

Wait until you have become joined in marriage, with the one you have chosen to love and to give yourself, before you enter into a sexual relationship. Don't expose your body to the risk of disease and unplanned pregnancies. Don't become all used up, losing respect for yourself and destroying the beauty of the sexual experience because you give yourself freely to anyone who asks. These ideals may sound old-fashioned, but they still make good sense, even in a day when sexual intercourse on the first date can be commonplace.

Stay away from chemicals that eat away at the tissues of your very flesh and bone. Drugs and strong drink kill healthy cells. They have no place in God's temple.

Instead of seeking ways to damage your body, as so many people do today, find ways to strengthen it: eat healthful foods, exercise, rest, avoid harmful drugs, practice safety. Consider your body a gracious gift from God to you.

Paul went one step further in his "body language." "I appeal to you therefore, brethren, by the mercies of God, to present your bodies as a living sacrifice, holy and acceptable to God, which is your spiritual worship. Do not be conformed to this world but be transformed by the renewal of your mind, that you may prove what is the will of God, what is good and acceptable and perfect" (Rom. 12:1-2).

Seek to glorify God in your body. Keep your temple strong and pure, so that it can be a fit living sacrifice, holy and acceptable unto God. For, conforming to the values of this society, giving your body as a living sacrifice to the world, will do no more for you than it did for the young woman described at the beginning of the letter.

Love,
Mother

My Prayer for You

O Lord, may Alyce realize the value of her beautifully healthy body. May she treat it with kindness and concern. May she always be grateful to You for this precious gift to her.

In His pure love,
Amen.

Plucking-Up-Time

Dear Alyce,

One day, years from now, you will probably leave home and go to college. I have met many students in my lifetime. And, I've discovered that most of them consider moving from home and adjusting to a new environment (the college campus) a lonely, homesick, and frightening experience. To those first-year college students, I tell my "little plant" story. Since you may also face the trauma of going away to school, let me share it with you, too.

"For everything there is a season,
and a time for every matter under heaven:
a time to be born, . . .
a time to die;
a time to plant, . . .
a time to pluck up . . ."
(Eccl. 3:1-2).

Once upon a time
    a certain little plant
        realized
    it was
        potbound.
Once it was happy
    but now it felt
        unhappy
        discontented
        rootbound

living
    in the greenhouse
It yearned to learn
    of different grounds
        friendly greenery
        and other stems
    but . . .
        in other places.
So . . . the seedling
    plucked itself up
        out of the soil
        out of the stifling pot
        out of the greenhouse
    and moved far away
    to a different
        vessel.
At first
    our sprout seemed
        bewildered
        limp and lifeless;
    the new pot seemed
        big
        strange
        uncomfortable
        threatening.
Its leaves
    curled up
    and threatened
        to fall off.
Oh . . . it missed its
    old home
        the greenhouse
        warm

secure
familiar.
And . . . more than once
our sprout
thought of giving up
and going back
to its old
ground.
But . . . after a while
not yet throwing in the plow
our plant
made an effort—
wiggled its toes
in the new soil
stretched its legs
deep and wide.
And soon (but not too soon)
our plant
had come to love
its new bed
its new home.
You may be
like that plant
a growing seed
with
a growing need
to go away to college
to experience new things
to learn of different grounds
in other places.
God created
a big world out there
and somewhere

is *your* classroom
your locker
your bookshelf.
Growth demands
repotting
but . . .
repotting
does not mean
growth.
One must
sow and mow
in order
to grow.
Chances are
you may find
the college campus
unlike home
strange
uncomfortable
threatening at first . . .
strangers walking to and fro
and knowing no one
by his first name.
The thought of
going home
might cross your mind
more than once
and once more.
A home
a yard
a neighborhood store
things you knew so well
so familiar

so comforting
and now
so far away.
But wait!
Wiggle your toes!
Stretch your legs!
Feel the new soil!
This is
your classroom
your locker
your bookshelf.
Bury your roots
as deep as you can
for now.
And . . . one day
this big
strange
new campus
may indeed
become your new home.
But . . . we still have here
one very lonely bud
even in his
homey bed.
REPOT REPORT:
He misses
his hours with the flowers
his chums—the mums.
He is sad/homesick/blue
when he feels
the old dirt from home
still clinging
to his stem.

But . . . after a while
    he lets a little of the old
        mix
    with the new.
The former does not disappear,
    but mingles
        with the new.
Good, rich nourishment which
    turns his leaves
        a deeper shade of green . . .
            instead of blue
Which . . .
    helps his roots
        grow strong and firm
            the way the Gardener
                intended them to be.
His newfound friends
    the sunshine
        and the rain
    bless his new bed.
He holds his stem up
    straight and strong
Now . . . he is truly at home.
Loneliness hurts!
    All alone—homesick, very homesick.
    Those people
        so important in your life
        now many miles away.
So many students
    away from home
        for the first time
            take too much soil
            and hold on too tightly

to the old
to accept
the new.
And . . . we all know that
all old and no new
equals
no adjustment
to a different
way of life.
After a while
some let old traditions mix
with the new.
The former does not disappear
but blends with the new
and helps young roots
grow strong and firm
the way the Good Teacher
intended them
to be.
Good, rich nourishment
can come
from those we meet.
New friends can
richly bless
our new nest,
and make us feel
truly
at home.
Now . . . what about
our sprout?
Well, he finally became
strong
mature

happy
    in his new pot
    in his new home.
And . . . one day
    he looked up high
    to the sky.
And . . . opening up
    his tiny petals
      brought forth
        a lovely flower—
An inspiration
    for all to see—
      quite beautiful
      beyond degree.

                    Love,
                    Mother

My Prayer for You

O Lord, be near Alyce as she grows up and ventures into another stage of her life. May she look to You for strength and comfort when she feels all alone, homesick, and blue. Wherever You lead her, in selecting a college or career, may she bury her roots deep, lift up her head to You, and bloom there.

           In the name of the Comforter,
           Amen.

2

You and Your Home

"A good wife who can find?
She is far more precious than jewels.
Her children rise up and call her blessed;
Her husband also, and he praises her"
(Prov. 31:10,28).

Just What Can a Daughter and Mother Do?

Dear Alyce,
Just what can a daughter and mother do?
Some special things, just for us two?

We'll walk through nature, take trips, and hike,
We'll swim and run and play and bike.

We'll visit the tea rooms and have a nice lunch,
And friends will invite us over for brunch.

We'll cook and bake and plan holiday fun,
We'll shop for clothes and errands run,

We'll visit the sick and greet each with love,
And tell those we meet of our Lord above.

We'll read great novels, perhaps write them, too!
Take classes, and travel, and hobbies pursue.

And, when you are grown, our friendship won't end,
A new kind of love, no doubt, will transcend.

Just what can a daughter and mother do?
Some special things, just for us two?

We'll talk, we'll walk through life with each other,
Just you and me, daughter and mother.

Love,
Mother

My Prayer for You

My Father, I pray that Alyce and I will have many years to spend together.

In Jesus' tender love,
Amen.

The Super-Mom Myth

Dear Alyce,

One of these days, if you marry and have children, you may make the mistake that many mothers, including your own, often makes. We try to be super-moms!

What is a super-mom? She's a mother who tries to be 100 percent perfect in all that she does—and she tries to do everything, all at once. That's the best definition I can come up with.

Alyce, let me be the one to extend to you this truth: super-moms do not exist. At least I've never met one. No finite human being can "bring home the bacon, fry it up in a pan, and let her husband know he's a man" as the commercial suggests all at the same time. Time would not allow it. Energy levels would not allow it. The myth of the super-mom is just that—a myth!

I keep thinking that one of these days I'll be super-organized. I will become, in fact, a super-mom. Everything will be in its proper place, all the family's clothes will be mended, the house will be spotless, the trash will be tied up neatly waiting for the garbage truck, a week's meals will be stacked in the freezer waiting for the microwave, all the bills will be written and ready for the postman, the children will be clean—no runny noses, no dirty hands. I will look back over the house and say "Well done, Super-Mom" as I walk out the front door, dressed in suit, hat, and gloves, on my way to a writing assignment.

Well, anyway, that's my dream. The nightmare is what really goes on. The picture is more like this:

I walk out the front door on my way to a writing assignment, button missing from my suit, hat crushed by the cat, and one glove lost. As I shut the front door, I pray that no one will see the house before I can get home and clean it up. Dirty dishes clutter the breakfast table, baskets of dirty clothes wait for the trek to the washer, toys in the living room floor from the night before wait to be put away—well, you get the picture. This is reality around the George house.

No, I'm no super-mom, Alyce. My time and energy will allow me to do only so much, and then it's quitting time. Most nights, with supper dishes still stacked in the kitchen sink, I fall into bed, exhausted.

One thing I have learned though. I have learned to set some priorities. With the mountain of daily work and responsibilities, I've had to think through what's really important to me, and to us as a family.

What's really important?

You, little Alyce, and your brother, Christian, are important to me. Your daddy is important to me too. When I married your daddy, I made a commitment to love him. When your daddy and I made the decision together to bring you two into the world, we made a commitment to you too—to love you and to take care of you. That means making sure you eat right, get enough sleep, have quality medical care, have adequate clothes to wear, and other things that will affect you physically. That also means being concerned about your mental and emotional well-being—your education, your self-esteem. Your spiritual development is high on our priority list too. Our Bible reading, our praying together, our worshiping together—all these will help you build a strong spiritual foundation on which to base your life.

Loving you, caring for you, spending time with you, planning for your future, being dedicated to your growth and development—this is my priority as a mother. Loving your daddy, being sensitive to his needs, being a co-worker with him in parenting you—this is my priority as a wife. Next to these things, everything else takes a definite second place. In light of family members who love me and need me, how unimportant a spotless house seems.

Love,
Mother

My Prayer for You

Dear Lord,

Help my little daughter realize when she faces life as wife and mother and feels she must become almost super-human in her efforts to keep husband and children and home and career together that no woman can do everything herself, all at once. Give her the wisdom to set her priorities. Give her the energy to do what she believes is most important. And, give her the sense of responsibility to what she commits herself to do.

In His name, I pray,
Amen.

A Letter to My Mother

Dear Alyce,

Becoming a mother myself has made me realize even more fully just how much I appreciate my own mother. How often I fail to express my thanksgiving for her and my gratitude to her. Allow me to use this letter to you to pen a letter to her.

Dear Mother,

This thank-you note comes much too late, much too infrequently, and much too short to properly relay my love for you and my appreciation to you—my mother.

For the decision to have me, for the long months of carrying me, for the tedious hours of labor both *before* and *after* my birth, I thank you.

For seeing me through the terrible twos, the trying threes, and the even more trying teens, for supplying my every need, for nursing me through the mumps and the measles, I thank you.

For all the meals you've prepared for me, for the stacks of dishes and clothes you've washed, for doing the number of household chores I personally made for you, I thank you.

For taking me to school, for sewing my clothes, for the piano and the years of music lessons, for the lunches out and the shopping sprees, for our quiet talks, I thank you.

For making your career "motherhood," for giving up a job you enjoyed to care for me, for all the fun-filled freedom you've willingly relinquished, I thank you.

For being there to catch me when I fall—past, present, and future —for your loving support when I, myself, became a mother, and, for being my confidant and my friend, I thank you.

Love,
Your Daughter, Denise

Love,
Mother

My Prayer for You

O Lord, for my mother, I am grateful to You. For I now realize more than ever that motherhood is, indeed, a loving sacrifice. Motherhood brings unique joys, yes, but also sacrifices of time, energy, freedom, often career, and of self itself. No amount of money could buy the love and lasting devotion shown to me by my mother. I pray that, with Your help, I can be that kind of mother to Alyce.

In the name of my loving Heavenly Father, Amen.

When I Give Less Than My Best

Dear Alyce,

I gave less than my best at mothering today. Had I earned our living by "mothering," I would have been docked. It was one of those days: sibling rivalry, sibling and cat rivalry, crying, fighting, hitting—you name it, you and your brother did it! I spent my day in the "ring"—Denise George, referee.

On days like this, I feel I'm just not cut out to be a mother. Good mothers are made of more rugged material: denim, corduroy, and double-durable cotton. Today, I came apart at the seams. Like the short-lived polyester, I've been bent, stretched, and pulled out of shape.

I lack the qualities I see in so many other good mothers: patience, understanding, physical stamina, emotional endurance, wisdom, unlimited energy, and double-dosed kindness.

How quickly my patience runs out when my carefully delivered instructions go unheeded, and your brother continues banging your head with the Ping-Pong paddle.

Understanding: After a long day of continuous feedings and umpteen diaper changes, my understanding has faded into the woodwork. Today, I would quickly agree with the person who exclaimed in desperation: "Babies are ravenous appetites at one end and complete irresponsibility at the other end!"

My physical stamina and emotional endurance are strained by the early morning hours from lifting, stretching, bending, running, wrestling, carrying, and crawling.

Oh! for the wisdom of biblical Solomon. He must have been a very wise man because not only was he able to settle disagreements diplomatically but he also had other people to run his household.

Unlimited energy! This century's most renowned "expert" on family matters, Erma Bombeck, uses one word to adequately define parenthood: "exhaustion." My back agrees with her.

I realize that "a little kindness goes a long way" and that "you can catch more flies with honey than with vinegar." But, frankly, after the last bowl of spaghetti hits the floor, after the last drawer of silverware is dumped out, after the last mud pie is scraped from your and your brother's scalps, after . . . after . . . after . . . and, after . . . , my kindness runs thin.

So, little Alyce, if I have given less than my best to the awesome role of mothering today, forgive me. I'll try harder tomorrow.

Love,
Mother

My Prayer for You

Lord, for my lack of patience and understanding and a host of other motherly virtues for today and, no doubt, for many days to come, I pray Your forgiveness, Your understanding, and Your continued support.

In the Name of the One who has great patience
with me, His child, I pray,
Amen.

A Satin and Lace Wedding Dress

Dear Alyce,

My mother made my wedding dress. A long white satin gown, covered with rows of lace, and fastened by tiny pearl buttons, she sewed for months so that I would have a special dress on my wedding day.

Fourteen years ago, June 7, 1970, that event took place in my life.

I came upon my wedding dress today, sealed in a long plastic bag, in the back of my grandmother's upstairs closet.

Oh, the memories that flood forth as I carefully slip into the dress, smooth the lace, and button the tiny pearl buttons. (Yes, Alyce, to my surprise it still fit!)

Your father and I were barely out of our teens when we married on that Sunday afternoon. We had invited our friends and family and all the members of the Fellowship Baptist Church in Chickamauga, Georgia, where he served as pastor. The rain had poured on Chickamauga all week, until our wedding day. A sunny day in June, the church crowded with loved ones, I in my white satin gown, your father in his black suit, with my grandfather and the Reverend Sam Sharp officiating, we promised each other a lifetime—good times and bad, for richer for poorer, in sickness and in health, for all the days of our lives. We knew not what the future held, we only knew that we wanted to face it together.

I would not be truthful with you, Alyce, if I told you that your father and I have agreed on everything since that day. We've had our fair share of disagreements. And, we've known some pretty hard times—"for poorer" for sure! But, we've stayed together—"in good times and bad"—for the last fourteen years.

What has made our marriage a good and lasting one? Several qualities come immediately to mind.

A mutual love for Jesus Christ. Your father and I had each made a personal commitment to Jesus Christ before we met. After we married, we wanted to grow in our love for each other and together in our love for Him. Christ began as the head of our home, and He has continued to be the central part of our lives, both individually and jointly, ever since.

A spirit of teachableness. I call your father "my best teacher." He has taught me many things, among them a love for good books and literature. He has furthered my love of writing and of words as he noticed my undeveloped talents and encouraged the potential he saw. By keeping the lines of communication open, by mutually learning from each other, the years of our marriage has been a joint education.

Trust, love and respect. Your father and I have never given each other reason for mistrust in our marriage. We trust each other, we love each other, and we have a high respect for each other that forms the very basis for our marriage.

The ability to change and the ability not to change. A good relationship depends on flexibility—change—growing together, learning to live together, trying to please each other. Fidelity, on the other hand, means not to change—being true to the wedding vows. Infidelity is not only sexual unfaithfulness but any action that disrupts a partner's trust and confidence.

A spirit of unselfishness. Money, time, space, and life, itself, belong no longer to one individual, but must be shared eagerly and unselfishly with another.

Sensitivity. How often does your father respond to my needs before I voice them! Genesis states: "Therefore a man leaves his father and his mother and cleaves to his wife, and they become one flesh" (Gen. 2:24). I don't believe that that happens on the wedding day, but after long years spent together as husband and wife. Becoming "one flesh" evolves from a lifetime of love, mutual submission, and being sensitive to each other's most inward needs. For communication between loved ones seeks a higher plane than mere words.

Taking wedding vows seriously. Many men and women, especially in the last decade, enter into marriage with the idea: If it doesn't work, we'll simply end it. It's the "love at first sight, divorce at first fight" attitude. Surely God didn't intend holy matrimony to be approached in such a flippant way! Your father and I considered those promises we made serious business as we stood before God and spoke our vows to Him and to each other.

These suggestions do not nearly complete my list of "unsolicited advice for a good marriage." Kindness, sympathy, empathy, concern for those less fortunate, lack of jealousy, spouse encouragement, support, security, lack of fear, a willingness to understand, a listening ear, a helping hand—these virtues are also vital to our marriage. I pray, Alyce, that one day you will find someone you love deeply, with whom you can share all the days of your life. If you are wise, you will seek out a man like your father, another human being with whom you can share total commitment. And, on the day you promise yourself to him, I will hand lovingly to you this satin and lace wedding dress as my mother so lovingly handed it to me.

Love,
Mother

My Prayer for You

Dear Father,
I pray that You will bless Alyce's marriage as You have surely blessed mine.

In the name of the One who is perfect love,
Amen.

The Adopted Daughter

Dear Alyce,
How very special is the daughter who is chosen by two parents
who promise to love her
who promise to care for her
who promise to shelter her
who promise to nourish her
who promise to clothe her

who promise to educate her
who promise to teach her of spiritual things
who promise to laugh and cry with her
who promise to devote themselves to her
who promise to prepare her for life
who promise to see her through childhood
    into womanhood.
The gift of heart and hearth has been graciously bestowed on this
young chosen one. The gracious gift of love waits to be bestowed
on these loving parents.

Love,
Mother

My Prayer for You

Dear Father, bless those whom You, in Your infinite wisdom,
bring together as mother, father, and daughter. May their lives be
filled with thanksgiving at having found one another.

In Jesus' love,
Amen.

"Just Like Dear Old Mom's!"

Dear Alyce,
    Even though you've not yet lived one year, no doubt, you've
already discovered that I'm not much of a cook. The joke around my
kitchen is: "Where there's smoke, there's dinner!" Home cooking

has changed drastically over the last few years—about the same time fast foods became so popular. It has become crazy! The cooking methods I learned as a girl are surely outdated.

Now you can buy a frying machine that makes your homemade chicken taste just like it "came out of a Colonel's bucket"! Most every grocery store carries a brand of mayonnaise that transforms your made-at-home hamburger into a "Big Mac."

"Our french fries," one advertiser promises, "taste like they should come out of your oven in red paper bags."

Imagine the dismay of one grandmother when her three-year-old grandson turned up his nose at her morning's yield: baked sweet potatoes, roasted chicken, fresh green beans, and homemade ice cream.

"Why, what's wrong, Dear?" she asked, bewildered at her grandson's negative reaction to the lunch.

"Grandma," he whined. "Could I have a Whopper instead? That's what Mommy gives me when I'm real good!"

For some strange reason, Alyce, I've always considered fast food (that is grease—salt—white bread—sugar) something you served when you didn't have time to cook—when you were in a hurry. Grease, salt, white bread, and sugar are not my idea of a Sunday dinner, or any other dinner. Furthermore, why should any cook spend long hours in the hot kitchen trying to precisely imitate the latest in processed junk food? For heaven's sake, if her family wants chicken legs that taste like they are *in* a bucket, indeed, let them pull the chicken legs *out* of a bucket! If they want a Whopper, a Whaler, a Jack-in-the-Box, a McNugget, a Big Mac, or a McFish, let them go to the appropriate fast food chain, hang their heads out their car windows, and shout their orders into the life-size plastic clown's mouth. Then, eight-and-a-half seconds later, they can be thrust their "specially, carefully, handmade, designed-just-for-you-with-love" deluxe greaseburgers.

Who knows, Alyce, maybe one day things will really get crazy.

Can you imagine seeing a sign like this outside a fast food chain:
"Over twenty served daily! Our hamburgers taste just like dear
old Mom's!"

Love,
Mother

I Needed My Mother Most When . . .

Dear Alyce,
    I needed my mother most when
       I was a baby . . .
           Tiny, vulnerable, helpless
           Unable to feed myself
           Or keep my bottom dry.
           Unable to lower my fever
           Or speak my daily needs.
      My mother protected me, sheltered me, fed me,
           Washed me, and clothed me.
           She nursed me back to health.
           And, with her intuitive perception,
           She already knew my unspoken needs,
           And she cared for me.
    I needed my mother most when
       I was a toddler . . .
           Curious, adventuresome,
           Sometimes naughty,

And always seeking independence.
My mother sought to satisfy my curiosity,
And braced my constant falls.
She gave me loving guidelines
And allowed me a sampling of independence.
I needed my mother most when
    I was a young girl . . .
        Shy and awkward,
        Quickly growing up
        And not really wanting to.
My mother showed me the way to self-confidence
And assured me all little girls felt clumsy.
She helped make the "growing pains" less painful.
I needed by mother most when
    I was a teenager . . .
        Seeking answers to my questions,
        Making decisions about my life,
        And, fearing my advent into adulthood.
My mother answered my questions honestly.
And guided me wisely in my decisions.
She made adulthood seem
A less formidable stage of life to enter.
I needed my mother most when
    I became a wife . . .
        With new loyalties to house and husband,
        Striving to be a helpmate
        And seeking to blend two lives into one.
My mother taught me how to love and respect another.
She gave me a living example
On how to be a helpmate.
And, she showed me how to make a house into a home.
Nay . . .
    I needed my mother most when

I became a mother myself . . .
    Scared and exhausted,
    Overcome by awesome responsibilities.
My mother was there by my side when the baby came
And helped make the work a little easier.
She knew when to give advice
And when not to give advice.
And, through a lifetime of dedicated mothering,
My mother taught me how to mother.

                                              Love,
                                              Mother

My Prayer for You

Dear Father,
    I pray that I can be the mother to Alyce that my mother was to me. May that love and devotion be passed on to Alyce when she herself becomes a mother.

                    In the name of my Heavenly Father,
                    Amen.

One Plus One Equals Two Under Three—And Chaos

Dear Alyce,
    Your father and I waited eleven years for your brother, Christian, and another two years for you. During those long years, B.C. (Before Children), we had carefully organized our lives—a place for

everything and everything in its proper place. We were surely set in our ways! As I look back now, I wonder what we did with all of our time. Compared to our lives now, how unexciting our lives must have been then. For now, life is anything but *unexciting!* For we have your brother and you, and both of you are under three years of age! Needless to say, chaos rules!

I'm certainly not complaining, Alyce. We love you children. We thoughtfully and carefully chose the vocation of parenthood. We wouldn't change anything for the world. At the same time, I stand amazed, and somewhat amused, at how unorganized and hectically harried our lives have become.

Truly, one-plus-one-equals-two-under-three can cause certain commotion in the otherwise calm and tranquil lives of two set-in-their-ways, middle-aged adults.

Perhaps the hardest adjustment I've had to deal with is the constant interruption and continued chaos in the midst of highly sought-for organization. Chaos breeds chaos and interruption interrupts interruption!

Interrupting sleep, Christian's first shrill scream of the day announces to the family that he is awake and that we should be too. "I wake up! I wake up!" I look at the clock. Five AM. Your brother can't go back to sleep. So, the whole family gets up.

Chaos, mixed with at least one disaster, usually accompanies breakfast. All seems to be going too well as the family sits together and eats. That's when you or Christian drops a bowl of warm buttered oatmeal on the cat, who runs helter-skelter into the living room. As I rush behind the cat with a damp cloth, cleaning up oatmeal paw prints, the one of you who no longer has a bowl of cereal begins to scream at the one who does.

With breakfast over, your daddy, sprinkled with food, rushes to his early morning appointment at the office. (I can't blame him for making those appointments *early* in the morning!) You, Christian, and I begin the morning ritual of getting dressed. Only after I have disrobed both of you, drawn your bath water, and have towels and soap and shampoo ready for your bath, does the telephone ring. Someone tries to sell me a grave plot. I tell him I don't need one at the moment, but if this schedule continues, he might call back next week. Meanwhile, while balancing one naked baby on one shoulder and the telephone on the other, Christian has run out into the backyard wearing nothing but a smile. I chase after him, catch him, and bring him back into the house.

After the baths, after diapering two babies as they each try out for the 1992 Olympics, after getting both of you dressed, we begin the second meal of the day: lunch. Lunch proves somewhat consistent with breakfast. Food on the floor, milk on the table, both food and milk on your clean clothes. Another change of diapers, another change of clothes, a little sibling rivalry—hitting, biting, hair pulling —a few more telephone interruptions.

Your father usually calls us after lunch. "How's everything going there?" he asks in his most cheerful voice. "Just peachy," I answer in my most cheerful voice.

After lunch comes an interruption to the chaos and interruptions —naptime. My "rest." Trotting faster than any Kentucky Derby winner, I wash the breakfast and lunch dishes, make the beds, put out the cat, wash and iron the clothes, write out the bills, and start supper. The "refreshment" lasts only until the shrill small voice from the bedroom shrieks: "I wake up! I wake up!"

I won't go into what happens the rest of the day, Alyce. Every mother of young children knows. It's our quiet little secret that we don't often share lest someone think we don't enjoy the job of mothering. But you get the picture from the morning's schedule: more diaper changes, more clothes changes, more telephone calls, more mealtime disasters.

By the end of the day, as fatigue conquers its victim, the chaos takes on a more humorous note. How often I feel like the woman in the bubble bath commercial, who, (in the midst of the doorbell ringing, the telephone ringing, the children playing handball with the chocolate pudding, and the dog eating the supper off the counter) screams: "Calgon! Take me away!" I, however, am not instantly wisked off into a tub of creamy bubble bath surrounded by soft music. I must face the music, chase the cat, clean up the mess, and answer the door and phone.

"Maybe I'm just not organized enough," I mumble to myself as I empty the potty chair. "If I could become more efficient in my housework, more in control of the children, perhaps I could cut down on the day's predictable chaos." Then I recall the number of times your daddy has kept you. Complete chaos—wet diapers hanging from wet bottoms, cereal all over the floor, the frightened cat hiding in the cupboard, toys covering every inch of the floor—it's the same. Your daddy, however, has a peaceful and restful escape—a full-time job.

Little Alyce, you and your brother have been good for your father and me. You children are God's precious lesson to us in self-giving and concern for others. Parenthood has taught us that too much organization in life leaves little room for fun and spontaneity. It has helped us to develop a sense of humor. We often laugh at ourselves as we run to and fro and try to catch you pint-sized people or quickly move our toes as Christian, on his "hot cycle," and you, in your walker, turn our hallway into a race track. It has brought us closer to each other, as we sit down and examine the details of the day. And, best of all, we've learned to look at our days differently. We have blinked our eyes at the chaos and interruptions. For they are not important, they are only temporal. We now see our lives, and our rearing of you and your brother, in light of the eternal. Five, ten years from now, the chaos will be forgotten. (No doubt, other chaos will follow.) But we are doing something eternal here, something lasting. We are helping to guide two young children through childhood into adulthood. And that, Alyce, stretches into the everlasting, and goes beyond the moment's aggravations.

Love,
Mother

My Prayer for You

O Lord,

Allow us to look at the wet diapers and the spilled oatmeal as a necessary chaotic interruption in the eternal order of our lives. Help us to realize that the confusion, while certainly irritating, is small compared to the great vocation we have chosen—the nurturing and tending of our little ones.

In the name of my Lord, who understands,
Amen.

You Make It All Worthwhile

Dear Alyce,

I set off early this sunny Saturday morning while you and your brother were still asleep. With my list of errands in hand, and praising God for the beautiful summer day, I drove off to do the week's shopping.

Then, I met the world.

The grocery checkout lady, unspeaking and unsmiling, dumped my items carelessly into shopping sacks, looking at me only long enough to blurt out the amount of my bill. The man, waiting in line behind me at the fruit market, grumbled while the clerk rang up my fruit and vegetables. The department store saleslady spoke to me hatefully when I asked her a question about a shirt size.

It seemed that everywhere I shopped that morning, people were unhappy, uncaring, and complaining.

"What a day!" I exclaimed as I pulled into my driveway. "Thank goodness I shop only once a week!"

I stepped out of the car, laden with packages and sacks of groceries, and for the first time in hours, I saw a happy sight. There you were, little Alyce, with your brother, Christian, standing on the porch, eagerly awaiting my coming home. You had already extended your arms to hug me when I opened the door. My own little welcoming party, lovingly and excitedly ready to greet me.

And, that, little Alyce, makes going out into an uncaring, grumbling world all worthwhile.

Love,
Mother

My Prayer for You

O Lord, I pray that one day Alyce will have her own family to whom to belong. Give her the patience to face a world of unhappy people. Let her know that she has a home where she can find warm welcomes and smiling faces.

Thank You, Lord, for Alyce and Christian and Timothy—my family who makes coming home a restful pleasure.

In Jesus' name,
Amen.

You and Your World

"Let us love one another;
for love is of God"
(1 John 4:7).

Your Dad: The Bookworm

Dear Alyce,

If I could adequately sum up your dad in one word, it would definitely be *bookworm!* Webster describes a bookworm as "a person unusually devoted to reading and study." If so, your daddy is a bookworm with a capital *B!* Little did I realize when I married him some fourteen years ago, that my life would be filled with rows and rows of reading material. As I look around our home, I see the walls literally lined with cases holding these creatures.

While dating him, I lightheartedly understood his love for literature; but not until we married did I realize fully his intense passion for the printed page.

I kid your dad about spending our honeymoon at the Atlanta Discount Religious Bookstore. (I had wondered why he wanted to honeymoon in Atlanta!) He bought a trunk full of books and refused to leave them in the car. There I was, in the honeymoon suite, a brand new bride with my brand new husband—and all of Calvin's commentaries!

Over the years, I've learned to accept his studiousness. At the breakfast table, the lunch table, or the supper table, I no longer mind looking eyeball-to-eyeball at the back cover of a book, I've successfully adjusted to the bright reading lamp which hangs over our bed and burns long into the night (your daddy enjoys a late-night novel). But, I can't get used to what so much reading has done to your dad's everyday language. He no longer speaks in simple sentences.

("Good morning." "How is my family today?" "Pass the salt.")
Instead, he opens his mouth and proverbial quotes pour forth. ("Do
what good thou canst unknown, and be not vain of what ought rather
to be felt than seen." "He that raises a large family does, indeed,
while he lives to observe them, stand a broader mark for sorrow; but
then he stands a broader mark for pleasure too."[4] "Wit is the salt
of conversation, not the food."[5] That kind of stuff. Nerve-racking.

I've given up trying to do anything about his bookworm habits.
Hiding the set of encyclopedias didn't work. Throwing away thousands of yellowed *National Geographics* didn't help either. I've can-
celed morning newspaper subscriptions from all fifty states. That
didn't work either.

So, Alyce, if you ever happen to see a daddy-looking man reading
at a restaurant, reading at a meeting, reading at the library, or
reading at a red light, speak to him, he's probably your daddy—the
bookworm.

Love,
Mother

A Prayer for You

Dear Father
Thank You for Alyce's daddy.

Amen.

Your Granddaddy and Grandmother

Dear Alyce,

Let me tell you about my parents, Bob and Willene Wyse. You have met and spent time with them. Even though they live hundreds of miles away, I hope you will be able to spend much more time with them during your lifetime.

They are good to me. Both are dedicated parents who have always had my best interests at heart. Mom stayed home with my sister, Jill, and me for eighteen years. This was a career sacrifice for her as she left a good administrative position. Daddy always made a good living and provided us with a more than comfortable home.

I had a good childhood, one filled with happy memories. Let me share with you some of my remembrances of Mom and Dad.

Daddy could make fudge like no other daddy alive! Usually once a month, he would get a craving for the candy and announce: "Let's make some fudge!" I still remember our squeals of delight upon hearing those words. I can also still hear my mother's sighs which were two-fold—more pots and pans to wash and the caloric temptation.

Daddy made fudge the old-fashioned way—he cooked it. The smells of the bubbling rich chocolate filled the house. Jill and I were the fudge-ball testers. When Daddy thought the candy was ready to pour onto the well-greased waxed paper, he would drip a drop from the wooden spoon into a cup of cold water. When the candy formed a soft ball, it was ready. Waiting for the sheet of shiny fudge to harden on the paper was difficult, but Daddy made a good guard.

Sometimes the fudge turned out perfectly. Sometimes we had to eat it with a spoon.

Daddy made other things for us girls. He once built a playhouse. We woke up on Christmas morning, and there it was, all ready to move into. We were thrilled.

I hope, Alyce, that you will become good friends with your granddaddy. He's a fine man and a fine father.

Mom was an excellent seamstress. She made sure that not only did her daughters have beautiful clothes but that their Barbie dolls were the best dressed dolls in the neighborhood of make-believe. How she ever sewed those tiny bits of lace onto Barbie's evening clothes I will never comprehend. Barbie had an exquisite wardrobe, with matching jewelry, gloves, hat, and shoes, to assure proper dress for wherever Ken wanted to take her. Mom didn't stop with her attire. My Barbie and Ken even had monogrammed zebra-striped bedspreads to cover their shoebox beds.

Often since then, I've thought about the hard work Mom put into making those Barbie clothes. In doing so, she made me a very happy little girl.

Those are just a few memories I'll share with you, Alyce. I hope as you come to know and to love your granddaddy and grandmother they'll make for you memories you can also forever keep.

Love,
Mother

My Prayer for You

Dear Father,

Thank you for my mother and father, Alyce's granddaddy and grandmother. For giving me parents such as these, I am eternally grateful to you.

I pray that Alyce will come to love them as I do. May she also be blessed with bountiful memories spent with her grandparents. And,

may I, as a parent, bring to her the treasured gifts of remembrances
they so richly brought to me.
                    In the name of my Heavenly Father, I pray,
                    Amen.

Those Special People

Dear Alyce,
    How I wish families still lived together under the same roof—the
extended family unit. Grandparents, mothers, fathers, sisters, brothers, husbands, wives—one big happy "Waltonlike" family living
together and working together.
    Besides the constant company of loved ones, just envision the
treasures that you, the child, would gain from being surrounded by
so many family members who loved you!
    Since your birth, I have come to realize that two parents simply
cannot supply all the needs a child has. Some of your other needs,
whether emotional and/or spiritual needs, must be fulfilled by others as well as by us. "Lone Ranger" parents, who think they can
single-handedly rear a child from start to finish, are not being fair
to themselves or to the child.
    I can remember so many people who influenced me in my child-
hood. My own parents were my primary teachers, of course. But
what wonderful memories I hold from others who were instrumen-
tal in directing my future. Very early in my life, my grandparents,
Mama and Papa, told me of Jesus and His love for me. I believe my

desire to spend a lifetime in helping others is a direct result of their continued loving me and leading me to Christ. Many of my dreams for a family of my own came after the wonderful evenings I spent eating and talking with aunts and uncles and cousins and good friends. They all taught me about good family fun. As I grew up, I continued to reach out to others around me—old friends, new friends, schoolmates, fellow church members, co-workers. Perhaps the most influential person in my life is the person I married—your father. For the last fourteen years, he has truly been my best teacher and most cherished friend.

I could not possibly name all the special people is my life. Some are still vivid in my memory, and some I cannot recall by name. But, in their own time and in their own unique way, each of these special people has had significant gifts to offer me, treasures that will always remain with me. As I grow older, I realize even more the value of their teachings. I continue to seek out treasures of learning and advice from these and other special people.

So, Alyce, as you grow to womanhood, reach out to us, reach out to others, and be thankful for the gifts that all of us can give you.

Love,
Mother

My Prayer for You

Dear Father,

Even though Alyce's family is now spread out and separated by many miles, I pray that she will still look to them, as well as to us, to help fulfill her life's needs. From her Great-grandfather Williams may she receive the gift of a strong, enthusiastic, and everlasting faith. From the memory of her Great-grandmother Williams may she receive the gift of kindness, meekness, and devotion to family. From her Grandfather Wyse may she receive the gift of patience, skill, and generosity. From her Grandmother Wyse may she receive the gift of enthusiasm, ambition, and creativity. From other loved ones, and from the friends she will make over a lifetime, may she learn integrity, contentment, affection, loyalty, unselfishness, and a multitude of other virtues.

From you, dear Father, may she learn of the perfect peace and joy that comes from being Your child.

In Christ's name,
Amen.

Your Great-Grandmother's Death

Dear Alyce,

Let me introduce you to your great-grandmother, Alice Crane Williams. I must introduce you because you never had the privilege of meeting her yourself. She died on August 6. You were born on August 16. Only ten days interfered with the crossing of your paths.

Mama, as I lovingly called her, is special to both of us. She was my mother's mother. She was your mother's mother's mother. As I have already told you, I gave to you her name, Alyce.

Mama and I were as close as any granddaughter and grandmother could be. She was a kind, modest little woman who was totally dedicated to her family. I spent many happy hours with her during my childhood, youth, and early adulthood. When I married your father, we moved far away, making it impossible to travel the great distance home very often. But, even then, Mama and I wrote long, detailed letters to each other. I have saved all those letters from her. They number more than four hundred—one a week for more than seven years. She was extremely faithful in her writing.

Mama's last days on this earth were spent in pain and in and out of the hospital. At eighty-two, her body was tired. She had known pain and surgery and had faced death several times during her lifetime. On August 6, her heart and her lungs just stopped. I knew what to expect when the telephone rang at 2:00 on the morning of the sixth. Mama had died. "Mama is in heaven now," my mother, who was by her bedside, had told me.

I stayed awake the rest of the night. I prayed that God would be with the family, especially my eighty-four-year-old grandfather. I prayed that God would give me the strength to cope with her death. I had not lost someone I loved to death before. In my prayers, I thanked God that Mama was no longer in pain, that she was with Him and relieved of her suffering. I also thanked Him for allowing me to have my grandmother for so many years. Then I lay in bed and wondered what life would be like without her.

Our family rose as usual with the sun, but the day would be far from routine. Papa called and asked your father to bring Mama's funeral message. We quickly packed his suitcase and had the car filled with gasoline. Then, he was gone. Since I was heavy with you—you were to be born within ten days by cesarean section—the family agreed I should not make the trip. I spent the weekend at home, eyes swollen from crying, feet swollen from pregnancy and extreme August heat, trying to take care of your little brother, and hurting with the pain of loss.

That afternoon, my friend, Johnnie Sherwood, came over to be with me. She had heard about Mama's death, and she knew I was home with Christian. Her visit was a blessing to me. I will always appreciate her thoughtfulness.

I called the florist and ordered flowers for Mama's funeral service. Mama always loved flowers. She looked forward to each spring when she could plant her tidy rows of flowers in the yard. I selected lavendar and white flowers for her. In the middle of the spray, I placed a tiny pink rosebud surrounded by baby's breath. That was from you, Alyce, her unborn namesake.

I came face-to-face with myself in the midst of Mama's death. I discovered many things about losing someone you care for so deeply. Let me share some of these with you.

I realized that death will visit each of us. Perhaps more painful than realizing your own death is realizing the death of someone you love.

I no longer fear my own death. For, as my grandfather remarked, "Mama has broken the ice." When I die, I feel confident I will be in Mama's company.

My faith has been made stronger. I looked to God in my mourning, and He gave me strength. He gave me insight into the mystery of life and death. It was a confusing time for me. On the outside was Mama's death, on the inside was life—a baby ready to be born. I could not wallow in self-pity because I missed my grandmother. I had to get on with living. I had a baby to birth.

Mama, herself, helped me to accept her death. She loved life. She loved her family. She looked at death as a homecoming. When she passed on, she would be with Jesus. What a simple, yet profound, theology. She would miss her family here, but she longed to reunite with her family beyond.

After her passing, I realized how fortunate I was to have had so many special times with her. I will never on this earth have those hours again. I was thankful for each long-distance phone call I had made, regardless of the cost. I was grateful for each visit we had arranged to be with her, regardless of long hours commuting. For each word I had said, and for each word I had left unsaid, I felt glad.

I learned how important it is to have someone to love you. I talked to Mama a few days before she died. She could barely whisper, but I could hear and understand her words. "I love you, Mama," I told her as we were ending the telephone call. "I know you love me," she responded. Those were her last words to me. I loved Mama, and she knew I loved her. What a wonderful way to part ways.

Perhaps the greatest of all things I learned was this: The beautiful memories a loved one leaves behind keeps them alive forever. Mama's wisdom, encouragement, and loving ways will long continue to shape my life. She will always be a part of me. For when someone has lived the life that Mama led and leaves the wonderful memories that she left to me, she can never really die because she is very much alive in my memory. Through my remembrances, you, Alyce, will "meet" Mama, and she will become a part of your life too. I pray that she will have passed on to you not only her name but her kind, self-giving, and tender ways as well.

Let me share one last thought with you. Mama and I knew you would be a little girl. Medical science had made that news known. Mama also knew that you would be born on August 16, since Dr. Farmer had long before scheduled the surgery. Mama knew, too, that your name would be Alyce. So, had she lived to hear of your birth, you would have only confirmed what she already knew. She told me she was sorry she was too ill to choose a gift herself for her "little namesake." But, during our last hour together, when I thought she was too weak to get out of bed, she rose to her feet, walked to the dresser, opened the drawer, and tucked a ten dollar bill in my hand. "This is for Alyce," she said. "Please buy her something nice with it from me." Remember that, Alyce, whenever you look upon and cuddle the little china-faced doll from Mama.

Love,
Mother

My Prayer for You

Dear Lord,

Thank you for Mama's life and for the happy times we shared. Help me to remember every kind word, every wonderful story, every loving thing she did for me. Use me to impart her wisdom and tenderness to her "little namesake"—my daughter. And, even though Alyce and Alice never came face to face, allow me to introduce them to one another through a lifetime of precious memories.

In Christ's name,
Amen.

The Antique Box

Dear Alyce,

On top of the fireplace mantel in our living room sits a small antique box. I have no idea how old it is or where it was bought. It is a dull black, metal box covered with raised figures of grapes, vines, birds, and strange laughing faces. The fabric-padded interior blends together rich bright colors in an Oriental design.

My paternal grandmother, Louise, handed the antique box to me at our first meeting years ago. She had flown to Chattanooga from her home in California. Even though I was only five years old, I remember the introduction well. We sat together, my mother, father, and grandmother, at a table in the airport's dining room. All the while they sipped coffee and talked, I held my box delightedly and ran my finger along its intricate and unusual artwork.

I have cherished that little black box, Alyce. During the years of my life, it has been a temporary home for crickets, beetles, crayons, hair ribbons, autographs, love letters, and other prized possessions. It has followed me everywhere I've gone: Georgia, North Carolina, Tennessee, Massachusetts, and Kentucky.

Due to distance and busy work schedules, I've only seen my Grandmother Louise a few times in my life. But I have enjoyed her visits, and I always look forward with great eagerness to her next trip. Her husband, my paternal grandfather, died when I was six, before I had the chance to meet him. For that, I have always been sorry.

Being separated from parents and grandparents and great-grandparents is hard for me, Alyce. How I would enjoy having all my family members close by. You will also know the homesickness and loneliness you can feel for loved ones spread out across the country. We have no family members within hundreds of miles of us here. A visit once in a while, a letter or two, a long-distance telephone call, or a Christmas or birthday remembrance just doesn't take the place of a daily warm hug or a drop-by-the-house from those we call family.

How thankful I am for that little black box, Alyce. It will continue to go with me wherever I go—my cherished remembrance of the day I met Louise, my grandmother.

Love,
Mother

My Prayer for You

O Lord, for my paternal grandmother, I am thankful. I pray that Alyce will also have the opportunity to meet her.

Thank You for the priceless remembrance of the little antique box, Lord. For each time I gaze upon it, it brings back vivid memories of my grandmother and makes her seem a little nearer.

In His precious name,
Amen.

Snapping Green Beans

Dear Alyce,

How I loved to help my Grandmother Williams snap green beans when I was a little girl. Those warm summer mornings, so many years ago, come clearly to mind this morning as you and your brother sit on the back porch, and "help" me snap green beans for supper tonight.

The scene seems so much the same—the gentle cool breeze that rattles our sack of beans, the squirrels and birds bounding from tree to tree making their expected animal sounds, the laughter of neighborhood children several houses away. For a brief moment, I am whisked back in time to my grandmother's side on the back-porch glider.

With the large wooden bowl between us and a grocery sack on the ground beside us brimming with fresh green beans, my grandmother and I would begin our morning's work.

Back and forth we would rock on the old white metal glider. Surely, the comfort of this porch-version-of-a-couch could be compared to sitting on a rock! No doubt, the designer didn't get rich on this invention. Papa had painted the glider coat after coat over the long years it had been at home on their porch. At a certain point in the backward rock, the tired old glider would squeak. What could have been an annoying noise had become accustomed to, and long ago, no longer heard.

At my tender age, I considered snapping green beans serious business. I was proud to be my grandmother's "number one helper." It was a title I could boast about to the other grandchildren, for not many of them would give up a morning of play for what they probably thought to be "boring" business. I would painstakingly grasp the long green vegetable, pop off the pointed end (being careful to remove only the stem), pull the long string down one side until it reached the other pointed end. Then, I would pinch off that stem. With careful preciseness, I would mentally measure the bean to figure out into how many equal-sized pieces I could divide it.

"Am I doing it right, Mama?" I would raise my head and ask every few minutes, anxious for grandmotherly approval.

"Yes, Dear, just right." And then she would add: "You're such a goooood helper!" Then we would grin and go back to our snapping.

Snapping beans was fun, Alyce, but not necessarily for the actual pop, snap, and drop-in-the-bowl excitement. If nothing more than that, then it would, indeed, be boring business. The joy of snapping beans lay not in the *work* but in the *worker* who sat beside me. Rocking in the glider with my grandmother the whole morning and talking about anything and everything proved a handsome reward for the missed play. I knew that, unless a family member dropped by unexpectedly, which was usually quite often, Mama belonged to me for the morning. Selfish? Probably. But due to the geographical distance between us, our mornings together were rare. I realized, even as a young girl, that those quiet times with Mama were precious, never-to-be-repeated moments and that one day too soon they would come to an end.

This warm July morning, sitting in the porch swing with you, Alyce, and your brother, Christian, a wooden bowl between us and a little sack of green beans waiting to be snapped, brings back those truly beautiful memories.

"Am I doing it right, Mommy?" Christian interrupts my daydreams and asks me.

"Yes, Dear, just right," I answer, and then, remembering, I add:

"You're such a goooood helper!" Then we grin and go back to our snapping.

Love,
Mother

My Prayer for You

Dear Lord, may those precious quiet times I shared with my grandmother be repeated often with my children. May they enjoy and treasure them as much as I did with my grandmother, and as much as I do with them.

In the name of the One who makes all
of life's moments truly beautiful,
Amen.

"Good-bye": The Hardest Word to Say

Dear Alyce,
Perhaps the most difficult word in the English language is *good-bye*. It is a word we dread to say, but say it we must all throughout our lives to family and friends.

When your father and I left our families in Chattanooga and moved to Cambridge, Massachusetts, we said tearful farewells. Seven years later, when your father finished school and accepted a position in Louisville, Kentucky, we once again faced difficult good-byes. To neighbors, friends, church members, co-workers, and others who had exceeded friendship and had become almost family to us, we spoke our farewells and promised to "keep in touch."

Once we arrived at Southern Seminary in Louisville, we discovered that continuous good-byes would become an accepted part of our lives. Students, whom we would come to love, would finish their degrees, graduate, and move to different parts of the world. Each December and June graduation proved a time of celebration for the degree sought and finished but also a time of sadness for those who parted ways.

Alyce, you will soon discover that good-byes are, indeed, a way of life. Death of a loved one, a broken courtship, leaving home to marry, the moving away of friends, separation or divorce, graduation from school, a change of jobs, even passing from kindergarten to first grade—each involves saying farewell.

I have learned, Alyce, to enjoy and appreciate those whom I call friends and loved ones. For in this fast-moving society, we are usually together only a short time. Then we are separated and must spend our lives without.

Love,
Mother

My Prayer for You

O Lord, in this life we truly "meet and smile, and together walk a mile." Then we just as quickly part ways. Thank You, Lord, for those whom I've had the pleasure to meet and call my friends. I pray that Alyce will also meet those with whom she can "walk a mile" and call friend.

In the name of the One who never tells us good-bye, Amen.

Who Could Hurt a Child?

Dear Alyce,

Late last night a mother pulled her car off the highway and dropped her eleven-month-old daughter into a roadside ditch. Then she drove away. In the pitch black of the night, the scared baby girl crawled up onto the highway and was struck, by a car. She died immediately, alone, frightened, and forsaken.

Two weeks ago, a child-care center in California faced charges of child molestation among their enrolled preschoolers. The children were abused sexually, threatened, and frightened daily without the knowledge of their parents, who, in good faith, had chosen this supposedly superior day-care center.

A few months ago, a nineteen-year-old man, while babysitting for a five-and-a-half-month-old baby girl, brutally raped her. She was rushed to the emergency room, her condition described as severe.

I look at you, Alyce, my own beautifully innocent and vulnerable child and the question repeatedly comes to my mind: Who could hurt a child? What mother could throw her helpless daughter into a ditch and drive away? What teacher could sexually abuse and exploit an innocent child of two or three years of age? What kind of man could rape a baby? I can hardly believe that our society can be so very cruel to its children, both the unborn and the newly born.

How very much our Lord loved the little children, Alyce. When His disciples asked Him who among them was the greatest in the kingdom of heaven, He took a little child in His arms. "Whoever humbles himself like this child, he is the greatest in the kingdom of heaven," He answered them (Matt. 18:4). Then He gave a warning: "Whoever receives one such child in my name receives me; but whoever causes one of these little ones who believe in me to sin, it would be better for him to have a great millstone fastened round his neck and to be drowned in the depth of the sea" (Matt. 18:5-6).

For those who could hurt a child, Alyce, would that, even a great millstone, be punishment enough? Surely, the Lord must cringe each time one of His children is purposely harmed.

Love,
Mother

My Prayer for You

O Lord, be near those children who are hurting this very moment, those who are abused, mistreated, and forsaken. Erase their scars, Lord, ease their painful bodies and tortured minds, and give them rest in Your enduring love.

In the Name of the Lord who gives perfect rest,
Amen.

How Beautiful Is the Name—Grandmother

Dear Alyce,

Even in your brief life, you have already discovered this for yourself: How beautiful is the name—Grandmother. Let me tell you what my beloved grandmother meant to me.

How beautiful is the name
Grandmother
A woman who brings joy
To everyone she touches;
A parent who understands and forgives
The many blunders of childhood;
A keeper of precious memories
Who is always eager to share them;
A person devoted to those
Who call her "loved one."
How beautiful is the name
Grandmother!
A *Grand* and loving *Mother*—
Whose love for God
Only exceeds
Her love for her family.

Love,
Mother

My Prayer for You

O Lord, I pray that Alyce's grandmother, my dear mother, may bring those treasured gifts to Alyce that my grandmother brought to me.

In my Savior's name,
Amen.

How Beautiful Is the Name—Grandfather

Dear Alyce,

God especially blessed the children who have kind and loving grandfathers. He has certainly blessed me. The Lord has allowed my dear grandfather to live in good health for eighty-four years. Not only is he my grandfather, he's my friend. And, you already know that God has blessed you, too, by giving you your own special grandfather. Let me tell you what my grandfather means to me.

How wonderful is the name
Grandfather!
A tower of strength
When his loved ones need him;
A man of wisdom
From years of experience;
A person whose gentleness
Is displayed in every movement;
A parent whose kindnesses
Have blessed many young lives.
How wonderful is the name
Grandfather!
A *Grand* and loving *Father*—
The secure and sturdy cornerstone
Upon which a family is built.

Love,
Mother

My Prayer for You

Dear God, I pray that Alyce's grandfather, my own kind father,
may enrich Alyce's life the way my grandfather enriched mine.
In the name of my loving Heavenly Father,
Amen.

Of Loved Ones Past

Dear Alyce,

Not long ago, I came across your father's old family Bible hidden
on a dusty shelf in the attic. The Bible contained recorded names and
birthdates and death dates of the Georges since 1812.

"William George, Born May 1st, 1812, in Chichester, England.
Died July 31, 1884."

"Ellen McCormick, Born Sept. 3, 1819, in Grange County, State
of New York, United States of America. Died Oct. 22, 1897."

"Married in Rutgen Street Chapel by Rev. Dr. I. M. Knebbs.
William George to Ellen McCormick-on 27th August-1844, New
York City."

"Isabel Starr, daughter of William and Ellen George. Born in
Lexington, Kentucky on 30th July, 1845. Died at age 11 months."

"William Montell, son of William and Ellen George. Born in
Lexington, Kentucky on July 11th, 1847."

"Mary Francis, daughter of William and Ellen George. Born in

New York State, 27th August, 1849. Died aged 5 years, 1 month, and 7 days, May 29, 1855."

And, on and on the family recordings read, handwritten in faded brown ink on yellowed pages bounded by leather within pages of Holy Scripture.

Who were these people—an essential part of your father's past, and, Alyce, of your own past as well? What kind of lives did they lead? What were their occupations? How did they die—some still in infancy, others much older? Who took the time to so carefully record the events of their lives?

No doubt, that will remain forever a mystery.

They are all gone now. Fathers, mothers, daughters, and sons, who were born, who lived and married and bore offspring.

Our names will also be recorded in the family Bible one day, as we pass on to make room for others to follow.

Be grateful for those who came before you, Alyce, even though you will never know much about them. For through their births and through their lives, they supplied the family roots through which you came into this world.

Love,
Mother

My Prayer for You

Dear Lord,

May we give thanks to You for William George and Ellen McCormick and for their sons and daughters who also married and produced children. May we be grateful to You, may we be grateful to them, for their part in our lives even to this day.

In Jesus's name,
Amen.

Watermelon Memories

Dear Alyce,

Childhood flees. You are a young child now. I will turn to you tomorrow, and you will be a woman. I pray that between the short years of childhood and adulthood, you will glean loving memories to hold in your heart and in your mind long after the moment of childhood vanishes.

Let me tell you about some of my fondest memories as a young child. My "watermelon memories" are perhaps some of my most cherished.

Each summer, my sister, Jill, and I would travel to my grandparent's home in Rossville, Georgia. We would usually stay two weeks, unless our beggings to stay longer added another week or so.

During that fortnight, we would play outside and inside, sing with my grandfather around the guitar, visit our little cousins, and go to church and Sunday School and Vacation Bible School. We would also feed the dog, Little Man, and the horse, Inky, as well as the various other animals—an occasional goat, cat, rooster, or turkey—that my grandfather would invite to live at their farm.

The in-between play times—the rest times—were perhaps the most special to me. "Come get some watermelon!" my grandfather would call out loudly over the farm. Grandchildren, as well as some within-ear-range neighborhood children, would put down their balls and bats, climb off the swing sets, stop petting the horse, and would run quickly to the back porch. And, that's where it would happen!

While one of the grandkids held open the refrigerator door, (Papa kept his special refrigerator on the back porch), Papa would lift out a great, uncut, ice-cold watermelon. Then, as if to make us anticipate the ceremonial slicing all the more, he would slowly sharpen the long, worn, watermelon-cutting knife back and forth, back and forth until it was "as sharp as a razor." We would stand under a shade tree and watch him as he gently laid the watermelon on the backyard table and carefully eased the knife into its side. On a hot August afternoon, one can readily smell the rich full flavor of an ice-cold watermelon as soon as it is cut. He would then hand out the large pink pieces to each little waiting and eager hand, pass around the salt, and announce: "There's plenty more when you finish that piece!"

There we would stand, gathered around our grandfather and the quickly dwindling watermelon, spitting the seeds into the grass, the delicious pink juice running down our arms and dropping off our elbows. Hot and sticky, but inwardly refreshed, we would feed the gnawed-down rinds to the horse and return to our play.

How I miss those watermelon memories. Something happens when one approaches adulthood, Alyce. We can no longer so freely spit the seeds into the grass or allow ourselves to get sticky with the juice. Only childhood offers that ultimate freedom.

During my childhood, my grandmother and my grandfather provided memories both rich and abundant. I will always hold those memories securely in my heart.

I hope, Alyce, that your father and I, as well as your own grandmother and grandfather and other family members and friends, will enrich your life with watermelon memories of your own.

Love,
Mother

My Prayer for You

Dear God
Thank You for giving me grandparents who would take the time,

and who would love me enough, to provide me with such lasting, loving memories.

> With praise and thanksgiving, I pray,
> Amen.

A Letter from Your Grandmother

Dear Alyce,
   Your grandmother, Willene Wyse, is a significant person in your life. You already know her and love her. I have invited her to share with you in the following letter some of her thoughts.

> Love,
> Mother

Grandmother's Letter

Dear Alyce,
   What a beautiful name, Alyce! It stands for fairy tales (*Alice in Wonderland*), music ("Alice Blue Gown"), tradition (your great-grandmother's name), and, best of all, the present—Alyce Elizabeth George.
   Alyce, since your mom received a special box from her grandmother, Louise, I have decided to select a large oval box, paint a picture on the lid, and call it "Lil' Alyce Blue Gown Box." It will be for surprises and memoirs.
   When you come to visit me, it will always hold a special surprise for you. It will gradually be filled with momentos for you to have,

and it will be your own special box at "Grandmudder's" (as your brother, Christian, calls me).

When you get older and need a place for your own memory makers: pressed flowers, love notes, and so forth, the large box will find a new home—Alyce's bedroom.

Even before you were conceived, I had such a strong desire for a little granddaughter. There's a closeness between "us gals" that can't be denied or explained. I keep thinking of things I can share with you. It's wonderful being a grandmother. I have more time, more patience, more experience, and can, perhaps, make up for the mistakes I made with my own little girls.

You are such a precious little girl. You are centered in all my future plans. What have I ever done to be so blessed with such a little doll?

When I lost my own mother (your namesake) only a few days before your birth, I felt an emptiness that I knew could never be filled. But, then you came into my life, Alyce, and helped fill some of that emptiness.

It is my prayer that you and I will be as close as your mom and her grandmother, Alice, were. It takes love and understanding on both sides to build such a wonderful and lasting relationship. I hope I will always be there when and where you need me. You're my own special "Lil' Alyce Blue Gown!"

Love,
Grandmother

A Daughter's Daddy

Dear Alyce:

I'll never forget the first time I saw you, some four months before you were born. There you were, just a blurb on the sonogram screen: alive and kicking, scratching and turning inside the warm nest of your mother's womb. "Looks like you have a beautiful little girl," said the nurse. A girl! We were delighted and rejoiced.

Alyce, I am so glad that you are *you.* I cherish the special times we share together: sitting on the back porch listening to the rain, reading aloud your "How to Use the Potty" book, enjoying a picnic with Mommy and Christian in the park, hearing you try to sing "Jesus Loves Me This I Know."

Being a daughter's daddy is a unique experience. As we grow together in this relationship, I'm sure that you will have to teach me many things. No doubt there will be times when I disappoint you and misunderstand you. Times when I will disagree with you or even be angry with you. Bear with me, and, when you can, forgive me.

I promise to love you—no stings attached, to support you in every worthy desire which God places within your heart, and always to be there for you even when you stumble and fall.

Love,
Daddy

My Prayer for You

O Lord, thank You for allowing me to be the daddy of Alyce Elizabeth. Grant me the wisdom which such a calling requires. And bless my precious daughter. May she be as strong and loving as she is beautiful. Let our love for each other flourish and grow in the good spaces and times we will have together, until at last we have become, father and daughter, what in Your providence You have meant us to be.

> Through Jesus Christ our Lord,
> Amen.

You and Your God

"And Mary said,
'My soul magnifies the Lord,
and my spirit rejoices in God my Savior' "
(Luke 1:46-47).

Jesus Loves You

Dear Alyce,

As I sit and pen this letter to you, Christian, who should be taking a nap in the next room, sits in bed, plays his plastic guitar loudly, and sings for all the neighborhood to hear:

> "Jesus loves me, this I know,
> For the Bible tells me so.
> Little ones to Him belong,
> They are weak but He is strong."

(How could I interrupt such beautiful melodious theology to insist that he go to sleep?!)

Instead, I sit silently at my desk and listen to his mispronounced words and slightly off-key notes.

> "Yes, Jesus loves me.
> Yes, Jesus loves me.
> Yes, Jesus loves me.
> The Bible tells me so."

I remember the day we dedicated your brother to the Lord. We arrived early at church that morning. I dressed Christian in a long white baby gown—a gift from his grandparents—and tiny white lace socks. (How some of the ladies at the church chuckled at a boy in lace socks!) During the dedication service, we promised to seek prayer and divine guidance in his rearing and to dedicate ourselves to his spiritual upbringing.

We have taken that challenge seriously. I smile when I recall the day we brought Christian home from the hospital. Your daddy, so eager to begin Christian's spiritual education, slipped up to his bedroom carrying his new son clumsily in his arms. After a few minutes of missing them, I climbed the stairs and peeked into the room. There they were, a new daddy reading the Psalms from the German Bible to his new son.

"He can't understand German!" I kidded your daddy.

"Well," he replied, "at this stage, he can understand German as well as English!"

Ever since then, together we have sought to bring him up loving the Lord as much as we do.

Your church dedication was similar, Alyce. You wore the same long white gown, and, yes, the same tiny lace socks. I added a lace bonnet to your attire.

Your spiritual upbringing has received the same serious attention. Our family devotions each evening are simple: the Lord's Prayer, a hymn and a little chorus or two, and Scripture readings from the Psalms.

We have already introduced you to our Lord, Alyce. Through the years, we will help you to know Him better. For one of these days, you will come to a crossroads. You will have a life-changing decision to make—that of accepting Jesus Christ as your personal Savior and serving Him all the days of your life.

What sweeter words could meet our ears, child or adult, than these:

> Jesus loves me this I know,
> For the Bible tells me so.

As concerned parents, and with God's continued help, we will strive to do our part in your spiritual education. Just as we were nurtured in the faith by caring loved ones, so we extend that precious gift to you.

Love,
Mother

My Prayer for You

O Lord, You already know that You are no stranger to our household. We love You, Lord. Thank You for loving us. I pray that You will help us, as parents, to bring up Alyce knowing and loving You too. And, when she must make her decision as to who or what will be lord of her life, may she remember Your everlasting love for her.

In Jesus' precious name,
Amen.

A Woman in Crisis

Dear Alyce,

Someone once said: "We live in an atmosphere of crisis." No matter who we are, each of us will, at some point in our lives, encounter a crisis. You cannot expect a crisis-free life. Some people seem to be crisis-prone—as some people are accident-prone. Crises seem to follow them everywhere they go. I hope you will not be one of these people.

Crises come in various packages. Developmental and growth crises happen to everybody, all the time. Becoming a youth, getting older, getting married, having children—these are everyday crises and adjustments each of us will face. Crises that "knock us for a loop," that seem to make life almost stop for us, are called emergency crises. They also happen to all of us. These would include the death of someone we love, an unexpected illness, a divorce—that kind of thing.

Alyce, as a woman, you must also face crises, whether crises of growth or emergency crises. How you deal with these crises is important. How you cope with crises will say much about your person.

I have three suggestions for you as you prepare to cope with the crises that lie ahead of you. They all deal with strengths, and you must rely on all three to pull you through the expected and the unexpected.

Find strength in yourself. Be a strong woman. Become acquainted with yourself so well that when the unexpected occurs, you will anticipate somewhat your reaction to it. Learn to cry. Don't be ashamed to mourn deeply. Give yourself time to recover, and don't rush that time. But after the proper recuperation time, pull yourself together, and get on with your life. No doubt, others will be depending on you, whether they be family, friends, or co-workers. Work at building strengths from within, and draw from them when the worst happens.

Find strength in your family and friends. Alyce, I hope I will be around to offer strength to you in your times of trial. To have someone who loves you and understands you, who has known you from your infancy, and who will give you a strong shoulder to cry on is most valuable. Your father and I, as well as your other family members, will try to supply you with needed strengths. The friends you will make will give you strength when you need it, if they are indeed true friends. But that's a two-way street. For to have a friend is to be a friend. You must be there to help them when they need you.

Find strength in God. This is, of course, the most important source of all. If you have an ongoing walk with God, if you depend daily on Him for your strength and guidance, then how much more will you depend on Him when troubles overwhelm you. For God gives ultimate strength and power. Learn to depend on Him.

I hope, Alyce, as you live your life in the atmosphere of crisis, you will find these suggestions strengthening.

Love,
Mother

My Prayer for You

Dear Lord,

Protect my daughter from those crises that will upset her life and possibly even threaten it. I know everyone must face their share of crises, but I pray You will stand close to her in her times of need. May she always depend on You for her support and strength.

Be Thou my guide and my strength when, as her mother, she comes to me to receive an encouraging and uplifting word. I pray I will be there to help see her safely into womanhood.

For the strength You give me daily, I thank Thee.

Amen.

Love in a Casserole Dish

Dear Alyce,

When you and I came home from the hospital after your birth, we were greeted warmly by our friends in a way that touched our hearts. They came to the back door of our home bearing baskets of food: casseroles, salads, fruit pies, and cakes. People showed their love to us through the meals they prepared and gave. The giver of food represents the giver of nourishment. He or she shows genuine concern for a friend's or neighbor's bodily health and well-being—a sort of "I love you" in a casserole dish. Jesus, Himself, full of concern and compassion, broke bread and shared it with a multitude of people. The giving of food was one of many ways He showed His love for others.

I believe Christians show their love for their friends, families, and neighbors in no way more beautifully than in the sharing of their food. I know firsthand what gifts of food have meant to this family, Alyce. It involves work—in the buying of it or in the growing of it; time—in the preparing of it; and, an unselfish and loving attitude—in the giving of it. A loaf of homemade bread or a jar of homemade jam expresses a sentiment too deep for words.

If so much meaning can be placed in one small cake or pie or loaf of bread, Alyce, just imagine what we, as Christians, would express if our casserole dishes encircled the world! With thousands of people starving daily on our planet, and with many more millions going to bed hungry each night, we could show our love for Christ and our concern for our world's neighbors—next door and across the globe. How life-changing and life-sustaining this love in action would be!

Alyce, allow me to quote to you from Matthew 25:

"For I was hungry and you gave me food, I was thirsty and you gave me drink, I was a stranger and you welcomed me, I was naked and you clothed me, I was sick and you visited me, I was in prison and you came to me." . . . "Lord, when did we see thee hungry and feed thee, or naked and clothe thee? And when did we see thee sick or in prison and visit thee?" And the King will answer them, "Truly, I say to you, as you did it to one of the least of these my brethren, you did it to me" (vv. 35-40).

Truly, I say to you, Alyce, we have a loving obligation to the "least of these." Reaching out to them in Christian love with our food, the labor of our hands, is but one small part of what Jesus asks us to do.

Love,
Mother

My Prayer for You

O Lord, I pray that You will weigh heavy on my heart and Alyce's heart the plight of the world's hungry people. Help us to show more love and more concern for Your children everywhere. May we follow Your example and Your teachings. Through our money and our gifts, may we put our love into action—and into casserole dishes.

In His precious name,
Amen.

"Thou Didst Knit Me Together. . . ."

Dear Alyce,
Listen to these beautiful words in Psalm 139.

For thou didst form my inward parts,
    thou didst knit me together in my mother's womb.
I praise thee, for thou art fearful and wonderful.
    Wonderful are thy works!
Thou knowest me right well;
    My frame was not hidden from thee,
when I was being made in secret,

intricately wrought in the depths of the earth.
    Thy eyes beheld my unformed substance;
      in thy book were written, every one of them,
      the days that were formed for me,
        when as yet there was none of them (vv. 13-16).

Alyce, I remember well the day your father and I hurried downtown to the hospital. No, that was not the day of your birth. On this morning, through the magic of medical science (a sonogram), we would peek into my body and take our first look at you—our child. Your temporary home would no longer be secret, your privacy undisturbed.

The equipment in place, camera ready, parents eager, we saw you, curled up and nestled within your little home—warm, well-nourished, and happily comfortable, unaware of the journey you would be required to make within a few month's time.

"You have a perfectly formed daughter!" the nurse exclaimed, after careful examination. Healthy! Daughter! The announcement brought squeals of delight and thanksgiving from your mother and a hearty smile of relief and excitement from your more dignified father. A perfect daughter! We had hoped and prayed for that.

Then, you moved! Your tiny hand reached up to touch your face, and your thumb found its way to your mouth.

Your father and I marveled over you as we drove back home. You had some growing to do before delivery day, but you were a completely formed little girl. Our little girl. How we thanked God that you were ours.

"For Thou didst form my inward parts,
    thou didst knit me together in my mother's womb.
    my frame was not hidden from Thee,
when I was being made in secret" (vv. 13, 15).

When you were "being made in secret," long before we knew you, Alyce, the Creator knew you. When you seemed a mystery to us—the egg, the sperm, the conception—you were no mystery to Him. God formed you in the womb—He formed your inward parts —and He knew you, your character, your beauty, from your very conception. Then, He lovingly placed you in our care, for a time of incubation and growth, so that, nine months later, you would be ready to meet the world. Unborn, you were a little human being waiting to become a bigger human being. Since your birth, you are still a little human being waiting to become a bigger human being.

In her book, *Meditations for the Expectant Mother*, Helen Good Brenneman describes the unborn child: "Every baby is an immortal soul, a 'VIP,' a person created in the image of God. Even before birth the human fetus is precious . . . a Self, a Someone who will live on into eternity."[6]

On August 16, 1983, the day of your birth you held few surprises for us. For we had "known" you and loved you, our daughter, even as you were "being made in secret." Your unborn frame was not hidden from us.

Just imagine, Alyce, how well God—having formed your inward parts, having knitted you together in the womb—knew you and loved you. Indeed, how wonderful are Thy works!

Love,
Mother

My Prayer for You

Dear Father, thank You for the gift of our child. For all she meant to us before she was born, for all she has meant to us since her birth, we are deeply grateful to You.

In Christ's love, we pray,
Amen.

"Inasmuch as Ye Have Done It Unto. . . ."

Dear Alyce,

In Chelsea, Massachusetts, I often helped with the secretarial work in our inner city mission church. Located in the middle of a crowded, crime-infested area, I was approached routinely by some of the city's many "intoxicated transients"—referred to by Chelsea's residents as the "town drunks."

This day proved no different. This late Friday afternoon, I hurriedly tried to finish the end of the week's deposits. Before I could leave, a old man staggered up to my desk.

"Can I help you?" I asked, trying to be polite, but irritated at being interrupted and wanting to go home on time.

"Please, Miss, can I have some money to buy a cup of coffee?" he begged. He extended his hand toward me, expecting some change.

The stench of human body odor overpowered the room. The poor soul reeked with the smell of alcohol. Groping closer to me, he repeated his request.

After two years at the church, I had become accustomed to the many town drunks coming in and out of the building. I had given them money, brought sandwiches from home for them, had served them cup after cup of coffee, and had tried to put them in touch with agencies that could help them straighten out their lives.

Today, however, I felt unusually tired. I just wanted to finish my work and go home.

"No, I can't help you. I'm sorry," I told him. To justify my words, I assured myself he would probably just buy more liquor if I had given him some money.

He thanked me politely and walked out the office door. I watched him as he left, and, for the first time I really noticed him. He had a small fragile frame. An elderly man, his back was humped. His wrinkled skin reflected the many years of drinking and exposure to the weather. Twenty years out-of-style, tattered and worn, his clothes were hardly suited for the cool autumn weather. Slowly he made his way down the stairs, balancing his tired body on the handrail. He pushed open the front door, and, as quickly as he had appeared, he was gone.

Without wasting another moment, I finished the work and went home. I forgot the incident until later that evening. Even though I fell into bed exhausted, I could not sleep. The thought of the old man weighed heavily on my mind.

Could living and working in the inner city, where I saw so much suffering every day, harden me so much that I could not stop to help another human being? Was I no longer sensitive to the hurting of another? This man had stumbled to the one place he thought he could find help. Had the office work of the church become more important to me than the people of the church—those who so desperately needed ministering to? The thought made me shudder. I knew I had been wrong not to help this man.

Late that night, I whispered a simple prayer: "Lord," I pleaded, "please send that old man back to me and give me another chance to help him."

Autumn changed to winter. That winter set a record for being one of the most unkind of the century. The Lord did not give me a second chance, Alyce, as I had prayed. I never saw the man again.

Love,
Mother

My Prayer for You

Lord, teach us to take the opportunities You give us, when You send them, to minister to those who are hurting, those who need to hear of the One who loves them.

In Jesus' name,
Amen.

Every Able Body, Every Willing Soul

Dear Alyce,

"Time is short!" the apostle Paul echoed in his every sermon. Paul believed that the Parousia—the second coming of Jesus—would happen during his lifetime. Thus, he had much work to do in proclaiming the Lord's saving grace to the lost of the world.

The Son of God did not return in Paul's lifetime. Two thousand years later, we still wait for him.

On the eve of the twenty-first century, the Parousia grows even nearer. And, in light of the threat of nuclear holocaust, the world could very possibly be getting ready for the end of the age. Thus, we, too, must agree with Paul: Time is short! And, we, like the well-known apostle, have before us the Great Commission: "Go therefore and make disciples of all nations, baptizing them in the name of the Father and of the Son and of the Holy Spirit, teaching them to observe all that I have commanded you; and lo, I am with you always, to the close of the age" (Matt. 28:19-20).

I speak directly to you, Alyce, because one day you will be ready to choose or not choose Christ as Savior. If you become a Christian, as your father and I pray you will, you will also have a responsibility to fulfill, a commission to carry forth. Time is short, and you must join with other Christians in proclaiming the Lord's saving grace to the lost of the world.

Indeed, the Lord needs all of us—men, women, and children—every able body, every willing soul, to reach out and win the lost to Him.

Love,
Mother

My Prayer for You

Dear Father,

May Alyce choose Christ as her Savior and take her responsibility as a Christian seriously. I pray that she will look to You for leadership as she carries out Your commission to her.

In the name of the One who uses us
to reach out to all His lost children,
Amen.

Don't Worry

Dear Alyce,

How often do we as women give in to worry. Some women let worry and anxiety control their lives. They cannot cope from moment to moment without worrying. Many depend on antianxiety drugs to keep them going throughout the day.

We live in a dangerous and insecure world, Alyce. Perhaps worry will always be a part of this life. With the world's super powers ready to blast each other off the face of the earth at a moment's notice, we realize just how fragile this existence is.

As single women, we worry about our future, our career, our financial security. As wives, we may worry about our husbands—are they faithful to us, are they taking care of their health, what would happen in case of divorce or death? As mothers, we worry endlessly about our children, no matter how old they are. We are anxious about their health, their safety, their education, and our own role as parent to them. Women may worry about their larger family—their parents, sisters, and brothers. This is especially true as they relate to elderly parents and/or grandparents.

Yes, Alyce, worry is alive and very real for most women today. Some may find it hard to go to sleep, eat, or get up in the morning as they face unrelenting fears.

For the Christian woman, however, worry takes on a different meaning. We may have the same concerns that the non-Christian woman has, but we have Someone to help us cope with our fears. God can give peace to us as we seek it.

I can remember when your brother, Christian, was born. Oh! he was so tiny, so vulnerable. I thought if I touched him too hard I'd break him. I knew nothing about caring for a newborn baby. What was I supposed to do when he cried or broke out in a rash or ran a fever or coughed or sneezed? My mother stayed with me the first week after Christian and I came home from the hospital. But after she went home, I realized I would be totally responsible for this little creature. I will admit to you—I was one big ball of worry, fear, and anxiety! After several weeks of leaning continuously over his crib to see if he was still breathing, of calling the nurse with every anxiety that crossed my mind, and of staying up nights afraid he would die in his sleep, I finally came to a decision. I decided to give him to the Lord. I told Him that I couldn't be responsible for this little child all by myself. I had to have some help. I needed some peace about this new role of parent. And, peace He gave me. His sweet peace, which at that time did pass all understanding.

I can't tell you that I began instantly to sleep through the night, for Christian still wanted to be fed at two, four, and six AM. But I felt the anxiety ease. I would do my very best as a parent, I decided, and I truly believed the Lord would take over from there.

Peace. If He can give that kind of peace to a brand-new mother, He can give peace to anyone! Trust in Him, Alyce, with all your cares. Place your worries at His feet, and He will surely give you rest.

Love,
Mother

My Prayer for You

Dear Jesus,

I pray that Alyce will learn to depend on You, that she will bring to You her worries and her burdens. Give her Your perfect peace as she seeks to be a Christian woman in an anxious world.

In the name of the Prince of peace, I pray,
Amen.

The Worth of a Person

Dear Alyce,

Let me tell you about Ralph.

We met Ralph when your father and I visited friends in Germany. He had been invited by the host's son, a student at the local university.

Upon first sight, Ralph seemed rather out of step with the rest of the guests. He was a little ragged, in need of a haircut, in outdated clothes, and the soles were worn down on his shoes. He exhibited few social graces, and his table manners could have been improved.

Fifteen people sat and conversed around the great table that evening. Professors, students, family members, and Ralph joined together in the traditional German supper, the *Abendbrot.*

As we passed the chicken and cheese and homemade bread around the table, we talked about books just published, degrees recently earned, faculty positions open in various colleges—tidbits of great interest to those who dined. Things of interest to everyone —except Ralph.

Noticing that Ralph had not smiled or spoken all evening, the host, Dr. Mullman, shouting above the noise and laughter, asked: "And what kind of work do you do, Ralph?"

Embarrassed, Ralph tilted his head slightly toward Dr. Mullman and said almost in a whisper: "I'm a junk dealer, Sir. I collect and sell odds and ends here and there."

Ralph then quickly picked up his cup and gulped the tea. A silence fell over the room upon hearing Ralph's occupation. He blushed and silently focused his eyes on his dinner plate.

Dr. Mullman, sensing the young man's embarrassment, continued. "What kind of things do you sell, Ralph?" he inquired. "All kinds," Ralph said, still staring at his plate trying to avoid the gaze of the group. "From everywhere."

"Tell us a little about where you find these things," urged Mrs. Mullman, doing her part in the effort to make Ralph feel less ignored.

Reluctantly at first, then with growing enthusiasm, Ralph told us of some of his travels around the world in search of what he called junk. He told of the people he had met on his journeys, and how he, a Christian, had used every opportunity to tell them of Jesus' love. After a few moments of listening to him, we could clearly see that Ralph was somewhat of an expert on people and antiques. He described the people he had met and explained in great detail the history of the Chippendale chair, archeological discoveries in India, and all about the most exquisite Tiffany lamp ever found. He not only bought and sold antiques but also spent a good deal of time at the campus library researching them.

For the next half hour, all eyes were on Ralph. We listened almost spellbound as he spoke on a subject far more interesting than the previous ones.

Before the end of the evening, we had seen a shy young man with little self-confidence transformed in his own eyes. And, we all sensed that something revealing and intimate had taken place during the course of an ordinary meal.

I introduce you to Ralph in this letter, Alyce, because he has a valuable lesson to teach us about how we should regard others. At the end of the dinner, had Ralph not been encouraged to speak on a topic he knew well, we would have, no doubt, judged him primarily on his appearance and lack of social grace. How unfortunate that would have been! For, when we came to know Ralph through his past experiences and his future dreams, we found him to be a dedicated Christian man who felt a strong call to proclaim the gospel, a lover of people as he met and greeted them daily in his work, and an all-around, devoted student of life, anxious to learn everything he could about antiques. Ralph proved to himself, and to us, that evening, that he had worth.

As God's children, we should never have to prove we have worth. For we do, indeed, have worth. We are the ones for whom Jesus so willingly and so lovingly gave His life.

How often we judge others by the way they look or walk or talk, by the type work they do, or by the clothes they wear. Surely, we, the cruel and unfair judges, are the ones who miss the great opportunity to learn of one's heart.

Love,
Mother

My Prayer for You

My Father,

Whenever I am quick to judge a child of Yours because of the color of his skin, the style of her clothes, the shape of his body, or her table manners, forgive me.

I pray that Alyce and I, both, may learn to value others not for what they look like, but for what lies deep within their souls.

In the name of my Heavenly Father, who
knows the hearts of all His children,

Amen.

What Is Love?

Dear Alyce,

No doubt, the word *love* claims the title for the most misused word we speak. What is love? (You are bound to pose that question to me some day!) Perhaps real love does not dwell in what you say or feel, but in what you *do.* Christian love-in-action, then, holds even more meaning than love-in-action without Christ. The light of Jesus' love shines through His child and touches another in a unique way. Thus, love becomes something you do for someone else in the name of Jesus Christ.

Among numerous examples, here are my four favorite examples of that kind of love in action.

My friend is a bright, ambitious young man. He is married to a lovely young woman, and they have a baby boy. He studies at a prominent law school and has successfully completed his second year. Where does love fit into this example? Bill is blind. His devoted wife reads book after law book to him and accompanies him to class each day. She explains documents that she cannot understand herself and reads exam questions to him until her own eyes are bloodshot. She supports him in all ways possible. She has become his eyes. One could just envision them walking from class to class, her hand in his, leading him toward a life of helping others.

This, Alyce, is love.

I picture another friend, sitting by her elderly mother's bedside as her mother lies dying. Day by day, my friend watches her mother suffer from the cancer that is destroying her body. She has learned how to give shots and cries each time she must pierce her mother's skin to ease the intense pain. My friend gave up her own family life to care for her mother.

This, Alyce, is love.

Not long ago I was introduced to a woman who had devoted her life to God as a nun. She was an accomplished pianist and enjoyed this talent in the convent. She loved every minute of her work and had served faithfully for several years when she discovered she had multiple sclerosis. Slowly she began to lose the use of her muscles. Her hands were no longer strong enough to play the piano. Her legs would sometimes collapse beneath her. She felt she should leave her beloved convent, due to her deteriorating condition, so she gave up her life's dream. But being a person not easily discouraged, she became involved in a new kind of Christian work. She began helping poverty-stricken children to appreciate music. She worked endlessly, even while growing progressively weaker, and put new hope in the lives of underprivileged children.

This, Alyce, is love.

My fourth example deals with a perfect love, God's love. "For God so loved the world, that He gave His only begotten Son, that whosoever believeth in him should not perish, but have everlasting life" (John 3:16, KJV). It would have been easy for God to simply tell us He loved us. But instead, He proved His love through His Son, Jesus Christ. "God commendeth his love toward us, in that, while we were yet sinners, Christ died for us" (Rom. 5:8, KJV). He became one of us and willingly suffered to show us the way to the Father. Christ gave His life so that we might have eternal life through Him.

This, Alyce, is love.

                                                    Love,
                                                    Mother

My Prayer for You

Father, may Alyce's life be one of love for and service to Your children everywhere. May each act of love be done in Jesus' precious name,

Amen.

"You're Still My Baby!"

Dear Alyce,

Let me tell you about a talk I had with my grandmother a year or so before she died.

On that particular day, I had keenly felt the strain of motherhood and the fatigue of managing a house and budget. Everyday life just seemed more than I could cope with. I unburdened my soul as Mama, in her own understanding way, provided a listening ear.

"Mama," I confessed. "I wish I were a baby again and out from under this load of responsibility!"

She just looked at me knowingly and smiled.

"Well," she said, "you're still *my* baby!"

As always, her thoughtful words brought me relief. No matter that I had, thirty-two years hence, outgrown babyhood. I was still her "baby"! I belonged to her, and she loved me. What loving comfort those simple, yet profound, words brought to me.

You will probably also know of hard work, long hours, and mental, physical, and emotional stresses, Alyce. They seem to accompany adulthood. I hope you will come to me, as I went to Mama, with your yearnings to return to a carefree childhood. How I will look forward to repeating those lovely words to you: "You're still *my* baby"! For, no matter how many years you journey from childhood, you will always be my child. You belong to me, and I will always love you. I hope those reassuring words will bring comfort to you.

Perhaps we could make a theological point here too. How often do we turn to God in prayer when everyday life presents more than we can cope with. We want desperately to escape, even for a little while, the awesome responsibilities.

The psalmist felt this deep need for escape from his present situation when he cried out to God: "I am overcome by my trouble. O that I had wings like a dove! I would fly away and be at rest" (Ps. 55:2,6).

How often God speaks to us, answering our prayers with the comforting words: "You're still *my* baby"! No matter how troubling our situations in life, He stands ready to assure us that we still belong to Him, to His family. He promises to always love us.

What loving comfort those simple, yet profound, words bring to us.

Love,
Mother

My Prayer for You

My Father, thank You for the comfort You give us when we come to You in prayer. I pray that Alyce will always know that she is my baby, even when in the midst of trials. May we find blessed reassurance in knowing that we both belong to You.

In the name of our Heavenly Father,
Amen.

In Perfect Peace

Dear Alyce,

We come now to the end of the book. Throughout these pages, I have told you of many of my hopes and dreams for you. I've given you a glimpse of my own childhood, vague remembrances as well as vivid and life-changing experiences, that would have otherwise been unknown to you. You still know little of my life, Alyce, but I am and will be an important part of your life, as we journey together —mother and daughter—through each tearful, trying, and tender moment. I pray we will have many years together, you and I, to share, to enjoy, and to discover new hopes and dreams for each other.

Allow me to leave you with some parting wishes—little "love notes," if you will, to carry in your heart throughout, what I hope will be, a long and consecrated lifetime.

I wish you health, happiness, success, hope, and peace.

Health: I pray you will strive to keep your body as strong and healthy as you are able. Good health is a gift, Alyce. Enjoy every day that you awake with a pain-free body. If you should fall victim to sickness or disability, turn to God, asking Him to help you bear the pain courageously. Take care of your body, mind, and spirit, for it is not yours alone—it is a precious temple that ultimately belongs to God.

Happiness: The world may promise you its happiness, Alyce, if you follow its ways. Do not listen. This is a false happiness, a roller-coaster happiness. For a moment or two, you may know laughter and thrills, but then, all too soon, the ride will be over, and you will have to step aside.

You can only find true and lasting happiness by knowing the Lord Jesus Christ and by being in the center of His will. The world does not know, and cannot compete, with this kind of happiness, Alyce. And, this is genuine happiness, one that will last a lifetime—and longer.

Success: How does society measure success? The same way that Mr. Webster does: "The attainment of wealth, favor, or eminence—a position of prominence or superiority."

How very differently the Christian may view success! Let me show you a true picture of success, Alyce. Mother Theresa of Calcutta, India, quietly goes about her work, telling all about the love of Jesus and caring for the starving and dying of India's "poorest of the poor." Praise and recognition mean little to her. Her rewards lie in picking the elderly up off the streets to give them a quiet place in which to die and retrieving babies "from the city dustbins" to nurture them to health.

How very far Mother Theresa lives from the wealth, favor, and eminence that this society terms success.

Hope: If you are a Christian, you have an eternal hope. You have a Heavenly Father who watches over you, who counts the very hairs of your head, who loves you, and who gives to you a blessed hope that lasts into eternity. Who, Alyce, could give you more hope than He gives?

Peace: No doubt, this world will never know peace. Humankind has the knowledge and power to destroy itself. With the hatred, lack of love and understanding, and violence that exists in the world, the possibility of self-destruction seems very real.

As depressing as this sounds, Alyce, I have good news for you. The believer in Christ can know peace—*perfect* peace. For Jesus promises us His own special peace: "Peace I leave with you; My peace I give to you; not as the world gives do I give to you. Let not your hearts be troubled, neither let them be afraid" (John 14:27). Learn of this peace, Alyce.

Dear daughter, in closing, here is my prayer for you. That you may trust in the Lord with all your heart, leaning on His strong arms to support you, turning to Him in your weakness, praising Him in your strength, seeking His counsel in your decisions, allowing Him to guide your every step, speaking to Him when you are lonely, singing praises to Him when you are cheerful, thanking Him for all that you are, and for all that you have, rejoicing in knowing Him, and in all things, being grateful to Him.

I leave you now with these inspirational words, written long ago by a master letter-writer:

"Rejoice in the Lord always; again I will say, Rejoice. Have no anxiety about anything, but in everything by prayer and supplication with thanksgiving let your requests be made known to God. And the peace of God, which passes all understanding, will keep your hearts and your minds in Christ Jesus" (Phil. 4:4,6-7).

Love,
Mother

Notes

1. Wayne E. Oates, *Your Right to Rest* (Philadelphia: Westminster Press, 1984), p. 80.

2. Ibid., pp. 11-12.

3. Ibid., p. 29.

4. Benjamin Franklin.

5. William Hazlitt.

6. Helen Good Brenneman, *Meditations for the Expectant Mother* (Scottdale, Penn.: Herald Press, 1968), p. 15.